Quranic
Wisdom

Quranic Wisdom

MAULANA WAHIDUDDIN KHAN

CPS International USA

First published 2015
This book is copyright free

CPS International USA
2665 Byberry Road, Bensalem, PA 19020, USA
Tel. 617-960-7156
email: cps@alrisala.org, www.alrisala.org

IB Publisher Inc.
81 Bloomingdale Rd, Hicksville
NY 11801, USA
Tel. 516-933-1000
Toll Free: 1-888-560-3222
email: info@ibpublisher.com
www.ibpublisher.com

Goodword Books
A-21, Sector 4, NOIDA-201301, India
Tel. +91-8588822675, +91120-4314871
email: info@goodwordbooks.com
www.goodwordbooks.com

Printed in the United States of America

Contents

Contents

Introduction

*I*f you read the Quran, you will find that it deals with all of the subjects relating to human beings. But the basic theme of the Quran is the creation plan of God. All other subjects touched on by the Quran are related to this basic theme, directly or indirectly. God Almighty created the universe, and, it is God Almighty who revealed this book that is called *Al-Quran*. The primary purpose of the Quran is to reveal that divine plan according to which the world was created and people were settled in it.

This theme, which is central to the Quran, is thus described in chapter sixty-seven, *Al-Mulk* (The Kingdom): "He created death and life so that He might test you, and find out which of you is best in conduct." (67:2)

Here the words "life" and "death" refer to two different periods of humanity. The word "life" represents the pre-death period and the word "death" represents the second period of life, which may be called the post-death period. God Almighty created man as an eternal being but he divided his life into two periods—the before-death period and the post-death period. The pre-death period is very short, about hundred years, while the post-death period has no such limit. It will continue for all eternity.

According to the Quran, God Almighty created an ideal world that is called Paradise. The present world — the planet earth — has all those things that man needs or desires. But, in this world everything is imperfect in its form. In Paradise, on the other hand, everything will be perfect and ideal. Paradise will be free of every kind of limitation or disadvantage. Moreover, Paradise is an eternal world. Paradise has a beginning but it has no end.

God Almighty created man and woman, bestowed them with freedom of choice and then settled them on the planet earth. Through His prophets, God Almighty gave guidance to humanity. In every age the prophets told the people of all races about right and wrong. They told them what was good and what was bad.

This was simply a piece of guidance: there was no compulsion for people to follow it. People were asked to develop their thinking in such a way as to bring about moral consciousness in themselves and to lead a good life by their own choice. In this sense, everyone is being tested. Then God Almighty established a system of complete recording. This recording system is managed by the angels. It is so comprehensive that it can record the intentions, the speech, the behaviour and the dealings of every single person. This system is operative at all times, day and night. The purpose of all these arrangements is to select the kind of men and women who deserve to gain entry into eternal Paradise. At the time of Doomsday, God will appear with His angels and according to the angelic record He will select those men and women who passed the test.

What are those qualities that are required for a person to be a deserving candidate for Paradise? In a single word, it is spirituality. Paradise is a spiritual world and only those men and women who have developed spiritual qualities in their personality will be blessed with entry into Paradise.

According to the Quranic description, "Paradise is the home of peace." (10:25). Paradise is a place where there is no nuisance, no noise and it is free of all kinds of pollution. The inhabitants of Paradise will be positive thinkers in the complete sense of the phrase. The environment of Paradise will be free of all kinds of negative states, like anger, malice, hate, revenge, wrong desires, jealousy, fighting, exploitation and dishonesty, for these negative factors cannot be part of the psychology of the spiritual inhabitants of Paradise.

The definition of spirituality given in the dictionary is—the state of being opposed to worldliness. This definition is partly true, for unworldliness is not just for the sake of unworldliness. It is for the sake of a higher goal. And that goal is to develop a spiritual way of life.

There are two kinds of spirituality—negative spirituality and positive spirituality. Negative spirituality means renouncing the material world, or leaving the society and settling in some jungle or on some mountain. This kind of negative spirituality has no creative role. It suppresses all the natural qualities of a human being, who then dies without having made full use of his natural potential.

Quranic spirituality is spirituality of the positive kind. It means living in the world and trying to derive spiritual food from material things as a matter of intellectual discipline. It means to control rather than kill one's desires.

The fact is that God Almighty has created a person with great potential. It is not good to suppress this potential. One should rather avail of this potential for the sake of personality development. It means experiencing all the goods and all the evils of society and trying to live with others without reaction.

Positive spirituality can be termed creative spirituality. For example, there is a verse in the Quran which says with reference to the believers that "they forgive people when they are angry." (3:134). It means that positive spirituality is based on the formula of anger management rather than on trying to become a person who has no feelings of anger. The formula for positive spirituality can be summarized thus: turn your negative sentiment into positive response; make friends out of enemies.

The formula for positive spirituality is based on the principle of simple living and high thinking. Simple living and high thinking are complementary to each other. Simple living saves you from all kinds of distractions and high thinking saves you from being the victim of negative experiences. Simple living and high thinking are a sine qua non of the spiritual culture.

Positive spirituality is mentioned as follows in the Quran: "You are on the sublime character." (68:4). Sublime character is that character which is based on high thinking.

If you read the Quran, you will find that it lays great emphasis on sabr (39:10), sulh (4:128), forgiveness (42:40), avoidance (7:199), contentment, and so on. Why all these teachings? These teachings apparently seem to advocate passivity. But that is not so, for they embody great wisdom. The Quran tries to build that kind of mind which is able to manage all the affairs of life on the basis of spirituality. It is not passivity that is advocated but skill in the proper management of life's problems. The purpose of this formula—indeed, it is the Quran's greatest concern—is to concentrate on high goals and one who wants to achieve high goals has no option but to foster the aforementioned qualities. He has to try to effectively manage all undesirable situations. Otherwise, he will become preoccupied by trivial issues and will fail to continue his journey towards higher goals.

In the chapter *Al-Shams* (The Sun) of the Quran, you will find these verses: "He who purifies it will indeed be successful, and he who corrupts it is sure to fail." (91:9-10). These Quranic verses refer to the importance of personality development, laying emphasis not on its physical but on its spiritual aspects. It is no exaggeration to say that this is the main theme of the Quran, personality development being its basic goal.

What is purification of the soul? It is to purify your mind of all kinds of bias and negativity. In other words, it is to de-condition your conditioning. This is the mind the Quran tries to build. One who fails in this de-conditioning process will become a corrupt or an unwanted personality in the divine scheme of things.

Man's personality is like an onion. An onion has a central core, but this core is covered by many layers. If you want to reach the core, you have to remove all these covers or layers. The same is true of the human being. A human personality is always subject to the process of conditioning, which wraps it up in many layers.

The process of conditioning begins right from birth. Initially, it is an unconscious process. The individual's family, his institutions, his society, and his community: all are sources of this conditioning. From childhood up to adolescence, he is affected by this conditioning. Only after reaching adulthood does he become able to understand this problem consciously.

From here onwards begins what is called personality development. It calls for an awakening of the mind and a conscious discovery of this problem. At this stage, the individual must develop the capacity for anti-self thinking. He must engage in introspection. He must try to de-condition his previous conditioning with complete objectivity. This is the most important task for every man and woman.

What is de-conditioning? It is a process of sorting out the items you have stored in your mind, all of which you must view with complete objectivity if you are to overhaul your personality in a dispassionate manner. You have to remove the negative items in your mind if you are to turn your negativity into positivity.

A man once asked the Prophet of Islam a question—a very comprehensive one. He said, "O Prophet, give me a master piece of advice by which I may be able to manage all the affairs of my life." The Prophet replied: "Don't be angry." (*Sahih al-Bukhari*, 6116)

This means that you must try to purify yourself of anger. Don't allow anger to become a part of your personality. It is only in this way that you can truly develop your personality.

The Best Story

❦

*I*n chapter twelve, the Quran narrates a story, which it calls 'the best of stories'. It is about the Prophet Joseph, who lived in Palestine with his father and stepbrothers. When Joseph was in his teens, his stepbrothers became jealous of him. They contrived to throw him into a dry well situated in a forest. But God came to his rescue—a caravan spotted him in the well and pulled him out. Later, they sold him as a slave in an Egyptian market. That was how he travelled from Palestine to Egypt.

"God does not waste the reward of those who do good, who are righteous and steadfast." (12:90)

Luckily his master was a courtier of the Egyptian King. As for his religion, the King was an idol worshipper, while Joseph, who belonged to the family of Abraham, was a believer in the oneness of God. After some years, when Joseph reached the age of maturity, he came in contact with the King. The King, greatly impressed by his personality and wisdom, offered him a high office in his government. In present terms, this was the equivalent of being the minister of agriculture. According to the Biblical narration, the Egyptian King said: "You shall be over my house, and all my people shall be ruled according to your word; only in regard to the throne will I be greater than you." (Genesis 42:40)

Joseph accepted this offer and successfully managed the agricultural affairs of the land at a time when there was a severe drought in Egypt and the surrounding areas. People became so happy that they accepted him as their hero. After narrating this story, the Quran says: "God does not waste the reward of those who do good, who are righteous and steadfast." (12:90)

What qualities did Joseph possess which elevated him to this high status? After reading his story, as given in the Quran, we can summarize these qualities:

1. Joseph's stepbrothers hatched an evil plot against him which was intended to cause his death. But Joseph never developed any kind of hatred or feelings of revenge towards them. Instead, he forgave them and gave them a warm welcome in Egypt, as mentioned in the Quran.

2. The caravan of traders sold him as a slave in the Egyptian market but he never protested against the caravan. He never said that he was a human being and that they were using him as a marketable commodity.

3. When in Egypt, he never created any problems for his master or the king.

4. He remained patient with the culture of idol-worshippers that was prevalent in Egypt at that time. Following the principle of avoidance of conflict, he availed of the opportunity given to him by the Egyptian ruler.

These were the qualities mentioned both in the Quran and the Bible, that helped him to rise to such a high status.

Honesty and Hard Work

The Prophet Moses was born in Egypt, where he lived for about thirty years. Then, for some reason he had to leave Egypt and after a long journey reached Midian (Syria). When he was resting under a tree on the outskirts of Midian, a very interesting incident took place which has been narrated as follows in the chapter *Al-Qasas* (The Story) of the Quran:

> And when Moses arrived at the well of Midian, he found around it a group of men watering their flocks, and he saw two women standing apart from them, who were holding back their flocks, so he asked, 'What is the matter with you?' They replied, 'We cannot draw water until the shepherds take away their sheep. Our father is a very old man.' So Moses watered their flocks for them; and returned into the shade and prayed, 'Lord, I am truly in need of whatever blessing You may send down for me.' And then one of the two women came walking shyly up to him and said, 'My father is asking you to come so that he may reward you for watering our flocks for us.' When Moses came to their father and gave him an account of himself, he said: 'Don't be afraid! You have escaped from those wrong- doing people.' One of the girls said, 'Father, hire him! For the best man to hire is someone strong and trustworthy.' (28:23-26)

Honesty makes one a trustworthy member of society and hard work means that a man is ready to dedicate himself to his work.

According to this story, Moses lived with his Midian hosts for almost eight years. His host, Shuayb, married his daughter to Moses; then after eight years Moses left Midian and returned to his homeland, Egypt.

What the woman said when she asked her father to hire Moses is the best formula for success in this world. It is a two point formula—honesty and hard work. Honesty makes one a trustworthy member of society and hard work means that a man is ready to dedicate himself to his work.

Being strong and being honest are two desirable human qualities. 'Strong' refers to physical strength and 'honest' refers to spiritual strength: both are equally important. One who has these two qualities can be described as a well-equipped person. These two qualities make one a super-achiever in this world.

There is a saying: 'God helps those who help themselves.' What is self-help? Self-help means to prove that you have these two natural qualities—honesty and the ability to work hard.

The First Murder

Chapter five of the Quran relates the story of two brothers, Cain and Abel. They were the sons of Adam, the first man to be settled on earth. For some reason a controversy arose between the brothers. After a heated exchange, Cain killed Abel. This was the first murder in human history.

Narrating this story the Quran says in the chapter *Al-Ma'idah* (The Table): "That was why We laid it down for the Children of Israel that whoever killed a human being—except as a punishment for murder or for spreading corruption in the land—shall be regarded as having killed all mankind, and that whoever saved a human life shall be regarded as having saved all mankind." (5:32)

This verse not only makes a legal provision in the case of a murder, but it also gives us an ideology of life which can be summarized as follows: Differences are a part of human life, you cannot eliminate them. So, if you have issues with other fellow human beings, don't become disturbed, but take them casually. Try to live with differences. Try to learn the art of difference management, either by ignoring the problem or by making some kind of adjustment.

In all situations, you have to accept in advance that confrontation or violence is not an option for you. It is completely out of the question. Be determined that you will opt for some kind of peaceful settlement, that you will never enter upon a course of action which could lead to violence.

Any violent action is like a boomerang. It acts against you just as it acts against others.

The killing of a person is not simply the elimination of an individual; it is the setting of an undesirable precedent, the effect of which will continue, directly or indirectly, to have a baneful influence upon all mankind. In this sense, every individual crime is a universal crime.

Violence is not simply a vicious solution to a problem. It is worse than that. It is a grave breach of ethical standards. Moreover, when you opt for violence, you are deviating from the path of self-construction. You are wasting your time and energy upon a non-productive course of action. In this sense, any violent action is like a boomerang. It acts against you just as it acts against others.

When a person opts for violence or murder, he does so out of anger. When one becomes angry, one becomes overwrought. This being so, one should not take a decision in such an abnormal state of mind. So when you are angry, keep your patience. Try to defuse your anger. Try to calm down. Take your decision only when you become emotionally normal.

Charity is a Duty

*A*ccording to the Quranic concept, the have-nots have their rights. The haves must give the have-nots their due, otherwise the haves shall have to pay a heavy price for their negligence in discharging their duties. Philanthropy is a duty rather than simply a charity.

An event narrated in the Quran in the chapter *Al-Qalam* (The Pen), is the best illustration of this concept:

We tried them as we tried the owners of a certain orchard, who vowed to harvest all its fruits the next morning, without saying, 'If it be God's will.' A calamity from your Lord befell the orchard as they slept. And by morning it lay as if it had already been harvested, a barren land. So, they called out to each other at the break of dawn, saying, 'Be quick to reach your orchard, if you want to gather all your fruits.' So they went off, whispering to one another, 'Be sure to stop any poor person from entering the orchard today.' They set out early in the morning, thinking they had the power to prevent. But when they saw it, they said, 'We must have lost our way. Indeed, we are utterly ruined!' The more upright of the two said, 'Did I not bid you to glorify God?' They said, 'Glory be to God, our Lord. We have surely done wrong.' Then they began to heap reproaches on each other. They said, 'Alas for us, our behaviour was beyond the pale. Maybe our Lord will give us a better orchard in its stead; we turn to Him.' Such was their punishment, [in this life]. (68:17-33)

When one gets a harvest, it is not the fruit exclusively of one's own labour. There are other natural factors involved in the harvest, without which no harvest is possible. So, nature also has a share in every harvest. And this share should be returned to those people who for some reason have suffered deprivation.

What are those natural factors? They are numerous, for example soil, water, bacteria, air, sunlight, etc. These factors are beyond the ability of the harvester to provide, but are externally made available by nature. So, nature has a share in every harvest. Philanthropy means returning this share to the have-not group. Those who pay this share will be rewarded by God, and those who fail in this duty will be punished.

The Quranic concept of philanthropy is based on the principle of equitable distribution of natural wealth.

The Forbidden Tree

The story of Adam and Eve is common to both the Bible and the Quran. According to the Quranic account, God created Adam and his wife, Eve and settled the pair in Paradise. Where was this Paradise? The Bible is specific on this point:

The Lord God planted a garden eastward in Eden, and there He put the man whom He had formed. (Genesis 2:8)

This was the beginning of the social life of man. God gave both Adam and Eve a basic direction:

God said, 'O Adam! Settle, you and your wife, in Paradise and eat freely from it anywhere you may wish. Yet do not approach this tree lest you become wrongdoers.' (2:35)

The 'forbidden tree', in one sense, was a symbol of social taboos. Breaking these taboos means involving oneself in social wrongdoing, as mentioned in the above Quranic verse.

When God created Adam and Eve, it was not just creating a pair, rather it was creating the first unit of society. Adam and Eve were not created to live simply as a pair forever but were destined to start a generation; and form a society complete in every respect, subsequently paving the way for the building of a civilization.

Anything that proves to be harmful to one's fellow men is wrongdoing.

Adam and Eve were given complete freedom but their freedom was a restricted freedom. They were to refrain from all activities which would go against their fellow men. In other words, they were forbidden to indulge in any kind of social wrongdoing, otherwise they would fail to fulfil the divine plan.

What is 'wrongdoing'? Anything that proves to be harmful to one's fellow men is wrongdoing. In other words, Adam and Eve were required to follow the well-known formula: You are free but your freedom ends where another's nose begins.

This was the first social lesson given to the first man. As well as having freedom bestowed upon him, man was created with great qualities and all kinds of infrastructure to allow him to make use of his talents. Thus man potentially was the master of his environment. He was able to create a world of his own, with the sole condition that he should not misuse his freedom. He must refrain from approaching the 'forbidden tree.'

If the members of society refrain from indulging in wrongdoing and all use their freedom within the prescribed limit, then in such a society everyone will be able to develop his personality. Moreover, this society will grow in every way for the better. Living in such a society is like living in Paradise.

Education Matters

*T*he first divine revelation received by the Prophet of Islam was the chapter of the Quran entitled *Al-'Alaq* (The Clot). It begins with these words:

> Read! In the name of your Lord, who created... who taught by the pen, taught man what he did not know. (96:1-5)

This was the first message given to the Prophet by God. It tells us that according to the Quran, learning has the greatest importance in human life. In fact, learning is basic to all our hopes and aspirations: the greater the learning, the greater the progress in life.

According to a tradition, one night in the year 610 A.D., the Prophet of Islam was secluded in the cave of Mount Hira. Suddenly the angel Gabriel appeared and said: 'O Muhammad, read!' The Prophet Muhammad being unlettered, said, 'I cannot read.' The angel again said: 'O Muhammad, read!' The Prophet repeated the same answer. For the third time, the angel said: 'O Muhammad, read!' But again the Prophet Muhammad said he could not read. According to the tradition, the angel embraced him and then he began reading the revealed words.

This story gives a great lesson: a lesson of struggle. It should be interpreted as meaning: Read even if you cannot read, learn even if you cannot learn.

This was the first piece of guidance given by the Quran. This revolutionized the minds of the Prophet and his companions, and they did their best to avail of every opportunity to acquire learning and education. This is illustrated by the following sequence of events.

After the migration to Madinah in 622 A.D, the Prophet of Islam and his companions were attacked by the Quraysh of Makkah. It was a one-day war, which was won by the Prophet and his companions. They were able to capture seventy of their opponents, who were brought to Madinah as prisoners of war.

Learning is basic to all our hopes and aspirations: the greater the learning, the greater the progress in life.

But the Prophet of Islam meted out no punishment to them. They were educated persons, by the standards of those days. The Prophet of Islam said to them that any one of them who would educate ten children of Madinah would have this service rendered by him accepted as ransom and he would be set free.

It was more than likely that these people might again start a war against the Prophet. But, judging by this incident, the Quranic message is that, even if you are unlettered, try to learn, and learn even if you have no teachers other than those with whom you do not have good relations.

All Men are Equal

After an unfortunate but significant incident in Makkah, the Prophet received a revelation from God Almighty, which has been recorded in the Quran in the chapter 'Abasa (He Frowned). The chapter begins thus:

> He frowned and turned away when the blind man approached him, for how can you know that he might seek to purify himself, or take heed and derive benefit from [Our] warning? As for him who was indifferent,

you eagerly attended to him—though you are not to be blamed if he would not purify himself—but as for one who comes to you eagerly and in awe of God you pay him no heed. (80:1-10)

The background to these verses is that, one day, the Prophet was engrossed in a conversation with some influential persons of Makkah, hoping to convince them—and, through them, the Makkan community at large—of the truth of his message. At that point, he was approached by one of his followers, Abdullah ibn Umm Maktum, who was blind and poor—with the request for a repetition or elucidation of certain earlier passages of the Quran. Annoyed by this interruption of what he momentarily regarded as a more important endeavour, the Prophet "frowned and turned away" from the blind man—and was immediately, there and then, reproved by the revelation of the first ten verses of this chapter. In later years he often greeted Ibn Umm Maktum with these words of humility: "Welcome to him on whose account God has rebuked me!"

All men and women are equal in the eyes of God. If there is any difference, it is only between the Creator and His creatures.

This incident, recorded in the Quran, teaches the universal lesson that every human being is worthy of respect and should be treated on an equal basis, regardless of whether he is poor or rich, a common man or a highly placed person.

All men and women are equal in the eyes of God. If there is any difference, it is only between the Creator and His creatures. As far as God's creatures are concerned, everyone enjoys the same status and respect and deserves to receive the same importance.

Equality is not simply a moral value, it is more than that.

Equality means equal regard, equal opportunities, equal freedom, equal right to development and progress.

Muhammad was a Prophet of God, but in terms of equality, the Quran did not differentiate between the Prophet and a common man. Equality has an absolute value in the Islamic system. No compromise whatsoever is allowed in this regard.

Animals as Teachers

According to the Quran, Cain and Abel were the first sons of Adam and Eve. As the result of a controversy which arose between the two brothers, Cain killed Abel. One part of this story is narrated in the chapter *Al-Ma'idah* (The Table) of the Quran:

> When they both presented an offering, it was accepted from one of them and not from the other. The latter said, 'I shall kill you!' The former said, 'God accepts [things] only from the righteous. If you raise your hand to kill me, I will not raise mine to kill you... His lower self persuaded him to kill his brother, and he killed him and he became one of the lost. Then God sent a raven, which scratched the earth, so that He might show him how to hide the corpse of his brother. (5:27-31)

In this story the Quran depicts the raven as a teacher of man. This is not only an isolated incident. It has a general application. It teaches the lesson that in animal behaviour there are good examples for man. Man should study such behaviour and discover those good habits that are practised by animals and imitate them in his own life.

Why can animals serve as teachers to man? The reason is that man and animals both were created with the same nature, that is, following the good universal model for behaviour. But there was a difference. Man was given freedom of choice, while animals have no choice other than to follow the universal pattern. There are deviations in human behaviour but, in the case of animals, there is no deviation from the path of nature.

Due to this difference, man can be right or wrong but animals are always right. So, man should emulate the behaviour of animals in his life. This is the best way for man to stick to the straight path adopted by animals under the guidance of nature.

Man should study such behaviour and discover those good habits that are practised by animals and imitate them in his own life.

For example, tigers are the most powerful animals but they always avoid fighting. Jim Corbett, the well-known hunter, has rightly said that the tiger lives like a noble person in the jungle. There have been no wars in jungles such as World War I or World War II. Warfare is quite unknown in the culture of the jungle. A jungle sets the high standard which society must live up to if it is to be peaceful. Man must also follow this pattern of the animals. Every animal, big or small, provides us with a good example of social behaviour.

Social Etiquette

The Quran has given certain injunctions that ensure harmonious social living. One injunction of this kind is set forth in the chapter *Al-Nur* (The Light). The following is a translation of the relevant verses:

> Believers, do not enter other people's houses until you have asked their owners' permission and greeted them. That will be the better for you, so that you may be heedful. If you find no one at home, do not go in until permission has been granted you. If you are told to go away, then go away. That is more proper for you. God knows well what you do. (24:27-28)

These verses give the Quranic etiquette for social living. The Quran emphasizes and encourages good relationship between different members of society. But there are some principles which ensure a better social life and healthy and fruitful interaction. The principles given in these verses can be summarized as follows:

1. The first principle, in this regard is that, if you want to meet someone, you should fix an appointment in advance, so that the person can meet you without any reservation.

2. If you fail to make a prior appointment before visiting someone's home, you must on arrival knock at the door and wait to have permission from the occupants of the house before entering. Without permission from within, you must refrain from entering the house.

3. If you visit someone's home without a prior appointment and, after knocking at the door, you find that there is no response from within, you have to go away and return in due course.

4. If you visit a house without a prior appointment and are told by the occupants that at that particular time a meeting is not possible, accept this in a positive way and go away without any kind of rancour.

These principles are very simple and very practical. This is good for every society. These principles do not apply only to strangers but must be adhered to even by relatives and friends. These principles are common and universal. There is no exception to them whatsoever.

The spirit of these principles is that the members of society should be each other's well-wishers. They should try to avoid creating problems for others. Everyone should, from others' point of view, be predictable in character. All members of society must refrain from ill-feeling towards their fellow men.

Verify and Then Accept

*M*isunderstanding is a common phenomenon of social life. People tend to believe everything that is reported to them without scrutiny. And it is a common experience for reporters always to report things selectively or in a partial manner. It is selective reporting or partial reporting that creates problems. Sometimes people fall into grave misunderstanding and the result is disastrous. Chapter *Al-Hujurat* (The Apartments) of the Quran deals with this problem. It gives a clear direction in this regard. The translation of the relevant Quranic verse is as follows:

> Believers, if an evil-doer brings you news, ascertain the correctness of the report fully, lest you unwittingly harm others, and then regret what you have done. (49:6)

There is a background to this Quranic verse. When the Prophet of Islam established a state in Arabia making Madinah its capital, he sent one of his companions, Walid ibn Uqba, as a collector, to a tribe called the Banu al-Mustaliq. When Walid reached the tribal area, he saw that a crowd had gathered outside the town. He feared, due to some preoccupation, that the tribe wanted to kill him or beat him. After seeing this, Walid returned to Madinah, and told the Prophet that the Banu al-Mustaliq had rebelled and they must therefore send an army against them

Then the chief of that tribe, Haris ibn Zarar, himself came to Madinah. He said that they had gathered on the outskirts of their town only to receive the collector, Walid ibn Uqba, but that without meeting them, he had returned to Madinah. The above verse was revealed in the Quran after this incident.

By taking this example, the Quran gives the general direction that, before forming an opinion, we should scrutinize any news we receive. That is, before proper scrutiny, we should not accept its veracity.

Before forming an opinion, we should scrutinize any news we receive.

The principle to be followed is that if you are going to form a positive opinion, then scrutiny is not necessary. You can believe that Mr. So and So is a very good person but, when you are going to form a bad or negative opinion about anyone, then you have to investigate the matter before forming your opinion. In such a situation, you have only two options: either to remain silent or, if you want to form an opinion, then you have to go into the matter in depth. Only then do you have the right to form a negative opinion.

The Supportive Role

According to the Islamic principle, all human beings, both men and women, are equal. Equality is one important principle of Islam. But it is also a fact that every man is Mr.

Different and every woman is Ms. Different. In such a situation, Islam gives a very practical formula—people are equal as regards respect, but they are different in the roles they play in life.

In every society, there are a few people who are born to play a primary role, while others are destined to play a secondary role. This is the law of nature. There is no escape from this natural law.

The Quranic chapter *Al-A'raf* (The Heights) refers to an instance of what happened when this law was flouted. The translation of the relevant verses is as follows:

Recite to them the tale of the man to whom We gave Our signs, but who then cast them to one side and Satan overtook him. And he became one of those who went astray—if it had been Our will, We could have used these signs to exalt him, but instead he clung to the earth and followed his own desires. (7:175 - 176)

In every society there is a person who plays the primary role, then there are other persons who play supporting roles.

These Quranic verses refer to a well-known personality of Arabia, a contemporary of the Prophet of Islam. His name was Umayya ibn al-Salt. He was known as an intelligent person and enjoyed a great reputation in the Arab society of that time. When he came to know that Muhammad ibn Abdullah claimed to be the Prophet of God, he became angry, because he thought that he, not Muhammad, should have been appointed as the Prophet. From this point onwards, he became hostile towards the Prophet of Islam and remained so up to the last moment of his life.

Citing this example, the Quran stresses the necessity for everyone to accept that in every society there are two different roles: the primary and the secondary. According to the law of nature, only a few people can play the former role. Others must willingly accept the latter.

A society can be run smoothly only when its members are ready to follow this formula of nature. In every society there is a person who plays the primary role, then there are other persons who play supporting roles. Both roles are equally important. Without following this principle, no society can have the status of a healthy society. This principle is a universal principle. It is applicable everywhere—in the family, in society, as well as in the government.

Avoid Confrontation

The first chapter of the Quran, *Al-Fatihah* (The Opening), was revealed in 610 A.D. At that time the Prophet of Islam was in Makkah. In this chapter the Prophet was given a direction from God to convey the message of *tawhid* (the oneness of God) to his people. This chapter begins thus:

> O you, wrapped in your cloak, arise and give warning! Proclaim the glory of your Lord; purify your garments; shun uncleanness; do not bestow a favour in the expectation of receiving more in return; and for the sake of your Lord, be patient. (74: 1-7)

At that time there was only one meeting place in the town of Makkah where the Prophet could find an audience—it was the courtyard of the Kaaba, a mosque built by the Prophet Abraham. But the people of old Makkah were idol worshippers and they had placed three hundred and sixty idols within the precincts of the Kaaba.

It would apparently have been necessary for the Prophet first of all to purify the Kaaba of these idols. But this kind of beginning would have been bound to create serious problems. It would inevitably have resulted in a confrontation between the Prophet and the idol worshippers.

So the Prophet resorted to a very practical method. He decided to ignore the presence of the idols in the Kaaba and just go to the audience and address them and convey to them the message of the Quran. The Prophet's formula on this occasion was—accept the status quo and avail of the opportunities that the presence of the audience afforded him.

This policy can be described as non-confrontational. It proved so successful that the Prophet was able to continue his mission for a further thirteen years without any confrontation. This policy is expressed in the Quran in these words: 'purify your garments.' In other words, purify the hearts of the people and leave the problem of idols until there is a change in the situation.

Accept the status quo in controversial matters and divert your activities to the non-confrontational field.

Our world is a world of conflict and differences. In such a world, there is a very important question: from where to begin? The answer, in the light of the above example, is to accept the status quo in controversial matters and divert your activities to the non-confrontational field.

The confrontational approach involves a very serious loss, that is, a waste of time and energy, while the non-confrontational method makes it possible to devote all your time and energy towards achieving your goal.

From Potential to Reality

❦

Abraham was a great Prophet. As a tribute to his greatness, he was called *Abul Anbiya* (Father of the Prophets). Born in ancient Iraq, he travelled to different countries, such as Palestine, Egypt and Syria. Lastly, he settled his wife, Hajira and their son, Ishmael in the desert of Arabia, in a place near present-day Makkah.

The Quran narrates the story of the life of the Prophet Abraham in different chapters. The above story is referred to in chapter fourteen. When the Prophet Abraham settled there, he said a prayer to God Almighty, which is recorded in the chapter *Ibrahim* (Abraham) of the Quran:

> O Lord! I have settled some of my offspring in an uncultivable valley near Your Sacred House, Lord, so that they may establish prayer. So, make people's hearts incline towards them and provide them with fruits, so that they may be grateful. (14:37)

One aspect of this story was purely religious. This aspect is quite well-known. But there is also another aspect to it that may be termed secular. The latter aspect of this story has also a great lesson to teach. And this is no doubt a universal lesson.

I would say that this prayer was not a mysterious prayer. It was the invocation of a natural law, that is, God created the present world with great potential and then He gave man the capacity to turn this potential into reality.

Four thousand years ago, when this event occurred, most of this area was a desert. This was the same area that is now in the broader sense called the Middle East. It is now a land where there is greenery, agriculture and horticulture, and where there are beautiful cities and modern infrastructure. Four thousand years ago all these things were hidden in nature. Now they have become a reality.

The story of the Prophet Abraham was primarily a religious story, but it showed that our world is so full of potential that even a desert can be turned into a green belt. This is a lesson which is universal in its application.

God created man with a great mind. But the creation was based on what is called in education the 'Discovery Method'. Everything was hidden in nature but it was required of man that he employ his mind to discover all those things. The history of civilization is an ongoing demonstration of this principle.

A World Full of Friends

The world is full of friends. Someone is your actual friend; another is your potential friend. You are living in a world in which there are friends all around. This is one of the universal concepts given in the Quran in the chapter *Fussilat* (Revelations Well Expounded). I would like to quote some relevant verses from the Quran on this subject:

> Good and evil deeds are not equal. Repel evil with what is better; then you will see that one who was once your enemy has become your dearest friend. (41:34)

These Quranic verses have a background. When the Prophet of Islam was in ancient Makkah, people became hostile to him and to his mission. The Makkan people used to abuse him and sometimes try to cause him physical harm in their show of hostility. Clearly, it was an undesirable situation for both the Prophet and his companions.

At this moment of crisis, the Prophet and his companions were given the above guidance. It meant: Don't show a negative reaction; don't be resentful; don't try to adopt the policy of tit for tat. Contrary to this, God Almighty revealed the above guidance, the essence of which was to keep one's patience, and to give a positive response in return for negative behaviour.

This formula worked very well. Very soon hostilities ceased altogether. The majority of those who had been hostile became the friends of the Prophet—first in Makkah and then gradually throughout the whole of the Arabian Peninsula.

If you read the Quran, you will find that almost all its verses convey the same positive message, either directly or indirectly.

Why did this formula prove to be so effective? The reason is very simple, good behaviour in return for bad behaviour has a far-reaching effect; it touches the conscience of others. And it is a fact that when you are able to touch the conscience of the other person, you will successfully change his heart. According to the law of nature, this behaviour is like a psychological compulsion; no one can afford to go against his conscience.

This Quranic teaching is based on a principle that may be called unilateral ethics. Bilateral ethics is not part of the social scheme of the Quran. There is no doubt that in terms of result, unilateral ethics is far more effective than bilateral ethics.

If you read the Quran, you will find that almost all its verses convey the same positive message, either directly or indirectly. The Quran tries to establish a society in which all its members, both men and women, adopt this kind of positive behaviour. Reactionary behaviour forms no part of the scheme of the Quran.

Like a Good Tree

According to the Quran, man must be like a good tree. A good tree is a natural analogy for a good man. The translation of the relevant verses from the chapter *Ibrahim* (Abraham) is as follows:

> Do you not see how God compares a good word to a good tree? Its root is firm and its branches are in the sky, it yields its fruit each season with its Lord's permission—God makes such comparisons for people, in order that they may take heed. (14:24-25)

The tree is a unique phenomenon of Nature; moreover, the tree sets an example for man. It is required of man that he translate this tree culture into human life. This culture implies being deep-rooted, vastly spread out and at all times giving out benefits.

A good man is one who is like a good tree. What is a tree? A tree begins from a seed, then it turns into a plant, then a strong trunk, then branches and leaves, and then flowers and fruits. A stone cannot grow, but a tree continually grows till it becomes completely lush green with many fine attributes, as referred to in the above Quranic verse.

The same is required of men and women. All men and women must develop themselves like a tree. Where the tree develops itself in physical terms, men and women must develop the same qualities in terms of morality.

Every human being should firmly establish himself on his roots; he should be strong like a tree trunk, he should have a vibrant character like the leaves, he should prove himself fruitful for society, he should convey to people positive vibrations of life, just as a tree supplies fresh oxygen to man, and he should provide shelter to his fellow human beings.

A green tree makes our world beautiful. Without trees, our Earth would be barren. A tree is a giver member of our world. It gives everything but on a unilateral basis. For example, a tree continuously supplies fresh oxygen but it never sends the bill for it. Similar behaviour is required of both men and women.

A good man is one who is like a good tree. A tree begins from a seed, then it turns into a plant, then a strong trunk, then branches and leaves, and then flowers and fruits.

Men and women must live in their society as giver persons. They must adopt this culture on unilateral basis. They must live in their society in such a manner that society may always benefit from them. Like this, men and women can make their society like a beautiful garden.

Self-Correcting Mechanism

Here are one hundred and fourteen chapters in the Quran. *Al-Zalzalah* (The Earthquake) is chapter number ninety-nine. There is a story relating to this chapter in which there is a great lesson.

It is said that once a man came to the Prophet and after some discussion, he accepted the Prophet's faith. Then the Prophet said to him: "Stay with Ali ibn Abi Talib—one of his companions—for your further training."

A few days later, the Prophet asked Ali ibn Abi Talib about the man who had come to him. He replied that he had stayed with him for a while and then he had gone away, and that now he had no knowledge of his whereabouts.

The Prophet said: "Anyone who meets him, bring him to me." After a few days the Prophet was able to meet him again. The Prophet said to him: "I asked you to stay with Ali ibn Abi Talib for your further training. Then why did you leave Ali?" He replied, "You asked me to take training from him. I did so and then I went away."

Man is accountable to God and every deed of man, big or small, will be evaluated by God.

Replying to a further question, he said that Ali ibn Abi Talib had taught him chapter *Al-Zalzalah* of the Quran, which says: "Whoever has done the smallest particle of good will see it; while whoever has done the smallest particle of evil will see it." (99:7-8)

Quoting these verses of the Quran, the man said that from these verses, he had found the complete message; so there was no need to stay on any longer with Ali. The Prophet asked: "How did you find the complete message in these verses?" He replied: "These verses tell us that man is accountable to God and every deed of man, big or small, will be evaluated by God. Then he will be rewarded for good deeds and punished for bad deeds. Now I always keep this in mind. I always do what seems good to me and I always refrain from what seems bad to me."

This story explains very beautifully how the Quran develops a self-correcting mechanism in every man and woman. The Quran wants everyone to be on his or her guard all the time. This concept is bound to make a person conduct himself properly. It is at the basis of a character-building system.

This concept inculcates a very strong incentive to always

behave well and refrain from bad behaviour in every aspect of life. This incentive works not only in public life but in private life as well.

The Importance of Time

Al-'Asr (The Passage of Time) is the one hundred and third chapter of the Quran. It is a relatively short chapter. Its translation is as follows:

> Time is a witness, that man is surely in a state of loss, except for those who believe and do good deeds and exhort one another to hold fast to the Truth, and who exhort one another to steadfastness. (103:1-2)

In this chapter the Quran refers to time. What is time? Time is a passing phenomenon; it is always in a state of travel, from present to future, from morning to evening, from today to tomorrow. Time is beyond your control, you can never stop time.

In making this reference, the Quran gives a very important lesson, one which is important for everyone, both men and women. This lesson is: take time as an opportunity. Avail of time before it passes away forever. If you miss the train of time, you will never be able to catch it again.

Al-Razi, one of the commentators of the Quran, says: "I was pondering over the meaning of this Quranic verse while I was in Baghdad. Why does the Quran say that time is a witness for man? Then I heard the voice of an ice vender. He was calling out to people, 'O people, purchase my goods before they melt away and vanish.'" The phenomenon of ice successfully explains this Quranic verse. Everyone's life is like a melting piece of ice. Every person is constantly losing his time. When he rises in the morning, he has lost the night, which cannot return to him again. As evening nears he has lost the day. By these verses, the Quran warns every human being to avail of time. Avail of the opportunities of the day that you will not get during the night, and avail of the opportunities of the night that you will not get during the day.

In other words, with these verses the Quran tells us the importance of time management. Time management is a must for every man and woman. We have a very short time here on this earth. In only a few years time, we will face death. Everyone should undertake a serious planning of his time in order to avail properly of his pre-death period. We have only two options before us, either to avail of the time wisely or face failure forever.

Only Givers Remain

In the chapter *Al-Ra'd* (The Thunder), the Quran narrates a parable illustrating the law of nature, that only those who prove to be giver members of society will be able to establish themselves in life. The following is the translation of the verse:

> He sends down water from the sky that fills riverbeds to overflowing, each according to its measure. The torrent carries along swelling foam, akin to what rises from smelted ore from which man makes ornaments and tools. God thus depicts truth and falsehood. The scum is cast away, but whatever is of use to man remains behind. God thus speaks in parables. (13:17)

In our world, material events symbolize moral realities. Whatever is required of man, according to the law of nature, is being demonstrated in the rest of the world at the material level, as in the two events of nature which have been described in the Quran. One symbol used is that of rainfall, with its water flowing and reaching rivers and streams. At that time a great deal of foam surfaces on it. Another symbol is that of silver and other minerals being heated in order to clean them, their impurities appearing in the shape of foam which, being useless for man, immediately thereafter evaporates into space. The main point which emerges is that the water and minerals which are useful to man remain intact.

> *The individual who has lost his capacity to benefit others has no place in this world.*

These are the natural events through which Nature shows symbolically what principles it has laid down for the success or failure of life. One principle is that, in this world, only those who prove useful to others will find a place in society. The individual who has lost his capacity to benefit others has no place in this world. The same is true of communities and groups.

The survival of the fittest, as a principle of organic evolution, is controversial but, as a principle of social life, it is quite tenable. Competition and challenge being integral features of every human society there are inevitably the ongoing processes of acceptance and rejection. It does not matter what you think about yourself. In social terms, you have to prove your ability to be a giver, otherwise you will be rejected by society. Society accepts only those persons or groups who prove to be a healthy part of it. This is an unchangeable law of nature, as described in the above verses of the Quran.

The Advice of a Wise Man

he thirty-first chapter of the Quran is named after Luqman. Luqman was not a Prophet, but he was a wise man. He lived before the advent of Islam, having been born possibly in ancient Sudan. He gave some advice to his son, a part of which is as follows:

> 'O my son! Though it be but the weight of a grain of mustard seed and though it be hidden in a rock, or in the heavens or on the earth, God will bring it forth... Say your prayers, and enjoin good, and forbid evil, and endure patiently whatever may befall you. Surely, this is something which requires firm resolve. Do not avert your face from people out of haughtiness and do not walk with pride on the earth: for, behold, God does not love arrogant and boastful people. Walk modestly and lower your voice, for the ugliest of all voices is the braying of the ass.' (31:16-19)

This advice can be summarized thus:

1. God is all-knowing; He knows everything, both hidden and open. This belief inculcates a strong sense of accountability in every man and woman. It motivates everyone to adopt a disciplined life and to follow the guidance of the Creator, because he believes that, if he fails, he will be punished by God.

2. Then there is prayer to God. Prayer is not simply a set of rituals; it is rather a way of acknowledging God's greatness. This acknowledgement makes one realistic and honest. This differentiates the human being from

the animal. An animal cannot demonstrate a sense of gratitude, but man does have this special gift.

3. It is also everyone's duty to be watchful of others and tell them about good behaviour and bad behaviour. It is an expression of well-wishing towards other human beings. An honest person cannot afford to live as an indifferent member of society.

4. Patience is a very important human quality; without keeping one's patience, no one can be good in his behaviour in life.

5. It is also required that everyone be determined, for without determination, no one can unflaggingly follow the path of truth.

6. The greatest minus point in an individual is arrogance, while the greatest plus point is modesty.

7. The ass has the bad habit of disturbing others. Man must refrain from this bad habit.

Successful Dialogue

*A*braham was a prophet of God who was sent to ancient Iraq. At that time King Nimrod of Babylonia had established a kingdom in the plain of Shinar, circa 2450 B.C The Prophet Abraham brought the message of *tawhid* (the oneness of God) to him. But the king refused to accept his message. A part of their conversation is quoted in the chapter *Al-Baqarah* (The Heifer) of the Quran as follows:

> Have you not heard of him who argued with Abraham about his Lord, because God had bestowed the kingdom upon him? Abraham said, 'My Lord is the

one who gives life and brings death.' He answered, 'I [too] give life and bring death!' Abraham said, 'God brings up the sun from the east, so bring it up yourself from the west.' Then the disbeliever was confounded. God does not guide the wrongdoers. (2:258)

This conversation between the Prophet and the king gives us a very important principle of dialogue. That is, if the response of the other party is not positive, do not follow the futile course of insistence. See the mind of the other party and adopt an alternative form of dialogue.

The best arguer is one who is not obsessed with his own mind but is able to see the other party's mind, which he tries to address.

When the prophet said that God Almighty was the Lord who gave life and brought death, the king said he could do likewise. This answer was wrong but the Prophet avoided repeating himself and, with a change of stance, he raised a different point. His second point was so compelling that the king became speechless.

This instance gives us a good example of successful dialogue. The best arguer is one who is not obsessed with his own mind but is able to see the other party's mind, which he tries to address. He changes his argument so that the other party may be brought to understand the point he is making.

It is a fact that there are different kinds of mindsets. Everyone sees things from his own angle. Everyone thinks in his own way. Everyone is obsessed with his own ideas. So, to convince the other party, you have to understand the mindset of others. You must try to address others' minds, even at the cost of making a change in your argument. This is the right way to have a successful dialogue.

When you see that the other party is not convinced with your argument, don't lose hope, change your argument and very soon you will find that the other party is ready to accept your point of view.

The Formula of Co-existence

he multi-religious society is a universal phenomenon, most societies being multi-religious in composition. A question commonly asked is: how to live in a society where believers of different religions are living side by side?

The Quran was revealed in the first quarter of the seventh century. Some of its parts were revealed in Makkah and some were revealed in Madinah. Both the cities were inhabited by people of different religions, namely Jews, Christians, and Muslims.

In this situation the Quran offered a very simple formula:

For you your religion, for me mine. (109:6)

This Quranic formula was based on a simple natural principle, that is, co-existence or mutual respect. This formula can be expressed thus: Follow one and respect all.

This formula is the only viable one in any multi-religious society, for it establishes instant peace. By following this formula, every religious group can find its due place without doing others any harm. It is a fact that peaceful co-existence is the only way of existence in this world.

Peace is the need of every religion. No religious activity can be carried out without peace, whether directly or indirectly. This formula, in giving room to all the religions in any society, ensures peace for all of them.

In the early history of Islam, there is a very relevant story in the life of the Prophet of Islam that aptly illustrates this principle. The Prophet of Islam migrated from Makkah to Madinah in 622 A.D. at which time there were some Jewish tribes living in Madinah. One day it happened that the Prophet of Islam saw a funeral procession passing through a street in Madinah. The Prophet was seated at that time. On seeing the funeral, he stood up out of respect. One of his companions said, "O Prophet, that was the funeral of a Jew, not a Muslim." The Prophet replied: "Was he not a human being?"

This means that the Prophet of Islam discovered a commonality between himself and that Jew, because both were men and both were created by God. Both had the same common ancestor; both were members of a universal human society. This commonality was enough to provide a basis upon which both could co-exist.

This formula of mutual respect is useful for all religious groups. By adhering to it, every religious group can flourish without any kind of confrontation.

How to Face Problems

The Prophet of Islam started his mission in the first quarter of the seventh century in Arabia—an age of religious persecution. The Prophet's mission was based on the oneness of God, while the people of that time were believers in idolatry. So they became hostile to the Prophet and he and his companions became victims of various kinds of problems.

It was obviously an unfavourable situation for the Prophet and his companions. At this critical juncture, God revealed a meaningful piece of guidance which is recorded in the chapter *Al-Sharh* (Comfort) of the Quran. This divine guidance is as follows:

So, surely with every hardship there is ease; surely with every hardship there is ease. (94:5-6)

In this Quranic verse the same phrase is repeated twice. From this repetition, the Prophet drew a very meaningful inference. That is, according to the law of nature, the situation of ease is double that of the situation of difficulty. So he formulated this principle: "Two situations of ease will surely prevail over one of difficulty."

The fact is that in every situation there are problems, but at the same time there are opportunities. This is a law of nature. But it is also a law of nature that the quantum of opportunities will be more than the quantum of problems. This being so, the best course to adopt is to ignore the problems and divert one's energy to availing of the opportunities.

Complaint about or protest against problems is of no value. Problems are not created by some person: they are a part of the creation plan of God. No one has the power to change the course of Nature. We have no option but to accept this natural course. The above Quranic formula is the only formula which it is feasible to follow in our world.

The best course to adopt is to ignore the problems and divert one's energy to availing of the opportunities.

So when you face a problem, don't be negative. Be normal. Don't be disturbed. Don't allow tension to develop in your mind. Simply assess the situation and, by avoiding the problem, try to discover the opportunities. Believe with complete conviction that there are enormous opportunities waiting for you—either hidden or open. So, set about discovering them, using all your mental powers and energy.

In such a situation, lodging complaints and making protests are nothing but a waste of time. Developing tension in your mind is only the result of your failure to understand the law of nature. So, be a realist and ensure your success.

Submission to God

*T*he Quran advocates the culture of spirituality. Quranic spirituality has nothing mysterious about it. It is a well-known discipline. It is only an alternative name for intellectual development. The formula for Quranic spirituality is expressed thus in the chapter *Al-'Imran* (The Family of Imran):

Become men of God. (3:79)

Becoming a man of God means adopting a God-oriented life. The God-oriented way of life is a complete way of life. It calls for the use of all human faculties. It means God-oriented thinking, God-oriented speech, God-oriented behaviour, God-oriented morality, etc.

Islamic spirituality is, in essence, God-centred and not self-centred. When you discover your Creator, you instantly establish communication between yourself and your Creator.

The God-oriented life is another term for the spiritual life. In this verse, the Quran uses the word *'al-rabbani'*. It means a spiritual person or a *rab*-oriented person. In fact, Islam is a religion of spirituality. It is a discipline that can be explained in terms of reason. Islamic spirituality is based on thinking.

Islamic spirituality is based on contemplation rather than meditation. It is mind-based rather than heart-based: it arises from the awakening of the intellectual faculty. When you think about the truth and you discover it, then you become a spiritual person.

When you ponder over the world around you, when your thinking goes beyond your immediate surroundings; you discover the truth that is beyond you, beyond time and space. You become conscious of yourself as well as your Creator. This is the beginning of the spiritual process in your personality and this process will continue to evolve.

Islamic spirituality is, in essence, God-centred and not self-centred. When you discover your Creator, you instantly establish communication between yourself and your Creator. It is like establishing a connection between the electric bulb in your room and the powerhouse situated outside your room. Just as the electric connection illuminates your room, so also does the divine connection illuminate your whole personality. Then you become *rabanni*, or a man of God.

The formula for Quranic spirituality is very simple—simple living and high thinking. Simple living prevents you from succumbing to distractions, thus allowing you to find more time to engage your mind in meaningful arenas. Simple living and high thinking are interdependent. Simple living gives you more time for high thinking, and high thinking makes you a man capable of simple living.

Spirituality is the essence of divine life; spirituality leads to a life where there is no tension, no negative thought. In other words, spirituality makes us positive human beings.

The Rise and Fall of a Nation

Everything that happens in this world is controlled by the well-known laws of nature. The same is true of the rise and fall of a nation. The Quran, in the chapter *Al-Anfal* (The Spoils of War), gives substance to this law thus:

> God would never withdraw a favour that He had conferred upon a people, unless they change what is in their inner selves. God is all-hearing and all-knowing. (8:53)

The same law is referred to in another Quranic chapter:

> God does not change the condition of a people's lot, unless they change what is in their hearts. (13:11)

By the word 'peoples' the Quran means the nation or society and by the word 'heart' or 'inner self' the Quran refers to individuals. Here, the Quran refers to that law of nature which determines the fate of peoples or nations. This law applies without exception to all nations.

According to this law, the destiny of a nation depends upon the individuals of which it is composed. Every individual is an important unit of his or her nation. If the individuals are good in character, the whole nation will be good, but if the individuals are bad in character, then the whole nation will become bad.

This law tells us how to reform a nation or a society after deterioration has set in. This law gives us the starting point. Whenever it has become apparent that a nation has fallen into evil ways, we have to start our reform from its individual members; that is the only possible way to begin. You can successfully address an individual mind, but you cannot similarly address a crowd.

This means that in such a situation we have to change individuals through education, both formally and informally. We have to change their minds and hearts, we have to change their way of thinking; we have to de-condition their conditioned minds.

Initially, every nation is a favoured nation. God is merciful to every group of people, but, with the passage of time, signs of degeneration begin to appear. Now the question is: what to do to regain the initial position? How to rebuild a society which has gone into decline?

The process of building a nation is like growing a garden. If you start by sowing seeds, you can grow a beautiful garden.

The answer is: begin from the beginning. Begin with individual reform. By addressing the individual, you can reach out to society as a whole. But if you start by addressing society in totality, you will not get anywhere.

The process of building a nation is like growing a garden. If you start by sowing seeds, you can grow a beautiful garden; but if you start with the garden itself, you will not reach your desired goal.

Practical Wisdom

King Solomon, who lived in ancient times, was the ruler of Palestine and Syria. He was also an Israelite prophet. One of his contemporaries was the Queen of Sheba, who ruled Yemen from circa. 1100 to 900 B.C. According to Biblical and

Quranic accounts, she received a letter from the powerful King Solomon in which he demanded that she surrender to him. What happened after she received the letter is thus recorded in the chapter *Al-Naml* (The Ants) of the Quran:

> The Queen of Sheba said, 'O Counsellors, an honourable letter has been delivered to me. It is from Solomon. It reads, "In the name of God, Most Gracious, Most Merciful, do not exalt yourselves above me, but come to me in all submission." Now advise me in this, Counsellors. I never decide any affair till I have conferred with you.' They said, 'We are strong and our prowess in battle is great, but the decision is in your hands, so consider what you will command.' She said, 'Surely, when mighty kings invade a country, they despoil it and humiliate its noblest inhabitants— these men will do the same.' (27:29-34)

Then according to the tradition, the Queen of Sheba avoided confrontation by opting for surrender. Thus she saved her country from invasion by Solomon's army. This surrender was only in the political sense; in all other senses she was able to continue to rule autonomously. The people of Sheba were a trading nation. By this partial political surrender, they were also able to continue trading as before.

Practical wisdom means: opting for the less than ideal when the ideal is not achievable.

This kind of act was not surrender, but a good example of practical wisdom. Practical wisdom means: opting for the less than ideal when the ideal is not achievable. King Solomon was very strong in terms of military power, while the Queen of Sheba was not nearly so strong. Moreover, the interests of her people lay in trading and not in developing their homeland into a military power. So by the strategy of a political surrender, which was of a partial nature, the Queen of Sheba was able to save her regime as well as her trade.

This practical wisdom is indispensable not only for rulers but for every individual, for controversy is a part of life. In the midst of controversy, everyone tries to produce an ideal solution. But the fact is that, in most cases, the ideal cannot be achieved. The best formula, therefore, is for everyone to opt for the possible. Don't run after what is clearly impossible or likely to have a disastrous outcome. That is what is meant by practical wisdom.

After Night there is Day

In the early period of his mission, when the Prophet of Islam and his Companions were in Makkah, they were facing great hardships that led to despair and frustration. It was a grim situation. The Companions started asking whether their mission had strayed into a blind alley. At this critical time, God Almighty revealed the chapter *Al-Duha* (The Glorious Morning Light). It reads:

> The glorious morning light is a witness; and the night when it darkens is a witness that your Lord has not forsaken you, nor is He displeased with you, and the future will indeed be better for you than the present. (93:1-4)

These Quranic verses refer to a phenomenon of nature. Due to the rotation of the planet earth on its axis, there is a constant succession of day and night. This natural phenomenon gives us a great lesson for our life. The succession of day and night symbolizes the succession of positive experience and negative experience.

In our life also there are dark nights and bright mornings, despair and hope, obstacles and ways out. These show that one should not become the victim of frustration by looking only at one's present. One must be hopeful about the future.

The present is temporary, like the night, and it is certain that after some days there will be a bright future. So, the best policy for a person is to work in the present and be sure that some day success will come and bear him aloft.

In the case of the Prophet of Islam and his Companions, this principle proved to be true in the complete sense of the word. In their present, they adopted this Quranic formula and then, in the later days, they achieved an unprecedented success in their mission.

The present is temporary, like the night, and it is certain that after some days there will be a bright future.

This law of nature is eternal; it applies to individuals as well as to groups of people. Individual success and group achievement are both covered by this common principle. Quite simply, this principle means: work hard in the present and be hopeful about the future.

Life is divided into two parts: the period of struggle and the period of achievement. The period of struggle is like night and the period of achievement is like day. Night certainly leads into morning, and this is true likewise of human life. One's struggle is bound to create a bright future. The only policy we are required to adopt is 'wait and see.'

The Real Achiever

*In the chapter *Al-Qasas* (The Story), the Quran records a story which has a great lesson for every man and woman. Qarun, or Korah, was a wealthy member of the Israeli community of ancient Egypt. When Qarun became arrogant because of his wealth, some of his community members told him that arrogance would not serve him well. According to the Quranic version the story is as follows:

> Korah was one of Moses' people, but he behaved arrogantly towards them. We had given him such treasures that their very keys would have weighed down a band of strong men. His people said to him, 'Do not exult in your riches, for God does not love the exultant. But seek the Home of the Hereafter by means of that which God has bestowed on you; do not forget to take your portion [of the Hereafter] in this world.' Be good to others as God has been good to you and do not strive for evil in the land, for God does not love the evil-doers.' But he said, 'I have been given it only because of the art I possess.' (28:76-78)

According to the Quranic account, Qarun was punished by God on account of his arrogance. This story enshrines one of the divine laws: if someone receives wealth, he should be grateful to God, otherwise he will be disgraced by God Almighty.

Any achievement in this world is due to two factors: (1) one's own efforts, and (2) the support of the infrastructure established by God in this world. The ratio is very unequal. One's own share is less than one per cent, while the share of the divine infrastructure is more than ninety-nine percent. This being so,

53

it is quite unrealistic for a man or a woman to become arrogant. The only realistic behaviour for an achiever is for him or her to show complete modesty.

Arrogance means denying the bounty of God and modesty means acknowledgement of God's contribution. According to the Quran, the arrogant should be punished for their ungratefulness and the modest should be blessed with greater bounty.

This, moreover, is directly related to personality development. Arrogance vitiates one's personality with negativity, while modesty creates positive thinking. There is a great difference between the two: negative thinking is the source of all kinds of evils, while positive thinking is the source of all kinds of goodness. Wise men are always modest in their behaviour.

Actions Matter

*A*t the time of the Prophet of Islam, there were certain people in Madinah who talked of the truth, yet they did nothing for its sake and used beautiful words to cover up their misdeeds. Exposing these people, the Quran says in the chapter *Al-'Imran* (The Family of Imran):

> Those who exult in their misdeeds and love to be praised for what they have not done should not suppose that they are secure from punishment; they shall suffer a grievous punishment. (3:188)

According to this divine principle set forth in the Quran, it is only real action that matters: empty words have no value in the eyes of God. Those who utter such words are referred to in the Quran as hypocrites. And hypocritical behaviour is not acceptable to God.

One who talks of the truth, yet does nothing for the truth, is guilty of falsity. He is trying to receive credit for something which he never did at all. He will be discredited before God; no credit will be given to him.

Why do some people speak like this? They do nothing but they try to utter beautiful words or write beautiful essays. These people try to please others—their audiences or their readers.

These people may be applauded by their audiences and elicit praise from their readers, but this kind of speech or writing has no value before God.

There are always people, both men and women, who can be fooled by false words but God Almighty, who is all-knowing, cannot be fooled in this way. According to the Quran, mere lip service—for example, just saying 'sorry' when a mistake is made, or saying 'thank you' when receiving help—is not enough.

One who talks of the truth, yet does nothing for the truth, is guilty of falsity. He is trying to receive credit for something which he never did at all.

When a mistake is made, you have to repent in your heart and when you are given much-needed assistance, you have to be grateful with all your heart and soul. Words are no alternative to deeds.

There is a great difference between social manners and real morality. Social manners are nothing but a self-deceiving practice; while real moral value is quite different, being based on great moral and ethical sensibility.

God Almighty grants His rewards only to those men and women who are honest and sincere; who are the well-wishers of others and who try to do something for them in a substantial sense and not simply for show. Never try to take false credit.

Law of Success

〜⚜〜

During the time of the Prophet of Islam, two battles took place in Arabia—Badr (624 AD) and Uhud (625 AD). In the Battle of Badr, the Prophet and his companions were the winners but, in the Battle of Uhud, they were defeated by their opponents. After the defeat at Uhud, some Muslims fell into despair. They said: "We were following the true path, so why did we suffer a defeat at the hands of those who had adopted falsehood in their lives?" At that time, God Almighty revealed the following verse in the Quran:

> And do not become faint of heart, nor grieve—you will have the upper hand, if you are believers—If you have suffered a wound, they too have suffered a similar wound. We bring these days to men by turns, so that God may know those who believe, and choose witnesses from among you; and God does not love the unjust. (3:139-140)

This observation set forth in the Quran at that time, also has a general application. It tells us of a universal law of nature, according to which success is not the monopoly of a single person or group. According to the law of nature, everyone is bound to experience both success and failure, sometimes one and sometimes the other.

It is usual for everyone to become happy when experiencing success and to become despairing when experiencing defeat. This kind of fluctuation is unrealistic. We must face both situations with a normal mind. We have to accept both the situations as being in the usual course of things.

This law of nature is not a random law. It is useful for every man and woman. It means that when you have success, you have to be grateful to God. And when you fail, you have to learn some lessons and re-design your plan after making a reassessment of the situation.

These twin experiences are common to all human beings, both as individuals and as groups. Those who are unaware of this law of nature fail to learn any lessons from either experience. But those who are aware of this fact will surely learn from these experiences, and then lead a life that is free of tension and negative thinking.

When you have success, you have to be grateful to God. And when you fail, you have to learn some lessons and re-design your plan after making a reassessment of the situation.

The ups and downs in life are subjects of management. Learn this art of management and both these experiences in life will prove to be good for you.

Blame Thy Self

The Prophet of Islam and his companions suffered defeat twice, at the Battle of Uhud (625 AD) and the Battle of Hunayn (630 AD). On the occasion of Uhud, they suffered total defeat and at Hunayn they suffered partial defeat.

At the time of both the battles, the opponents were the aggressors and the Muslims were the defenders. In both the cases, the Muslims were innocent and only the opposite party was to be blamed. This was the case in terms of justice and injustice. But the Quran, reviewing both the events, said nothing against the opposite party but gave advice to the Muslims, pointing out their weakness. In the case of Uhud, the Quran pointed out the lack of unity in their fold. The following are the Quranic words:

> And God made good His promise to you when by His leave you were about to destroy your foes, until you showed weakness and you disagreed among yourselves [concerning the Prophet's direction] and disobeyed it, after He had brought you within sight of what you wished for. (3:152)

In the case of Hunayn, the Quran pointed out the sense of pride which had erupted among the Muslims. Referring to this battle, the Quran says:

The only right thing to do is to engage in introspection in order to discover your own weakness and then to reassess your own planning.

Indeed, God has helped you on many occasions. On the day of Hunayn, when you took pride in your great numbers, they proved of no avail to you—for the earth, despite all its vastness, became [too] narrow for you and you turned back, in retreat. (9:25)

This is the Quranic way of thinking. According to Quranic teachings, if you face any kind of undesirable experience from another person or group, you should not try to protest against others or register your complaint against them. You should rather try to find out your own weakness, your own vulnerable point that gave the other party the opportunity to overcome you.

According to the creation plan of God, our world is a world of challenge and competition. In this world, success is not the monopoly of any individual or group. It is futile to indulge in complaints and protests against others. The only right thing to do is to engage in introspection in order to discover your own weakness and then to reassess your own planning. This is the only wise response to untoward situations. By self-correction, you can regain the target you failed to achieve.

Do not Provoke Others

During the Prophet's time, some of his companions used objectionable language against the gods of the non-believers. This resulted in a reaction from the other party. In this situation, God Almighty gave a very important piece of advice to the believers. This is recorded as follows in the chapter *Al-An'am* (The Cattle):

> Do not revile those [beings] whom they invoke instead of God, lest they, in their hostility, revile God out of ignorance. Thus to every people We have caused their actions to seem fair. To their Lord they shall all return, and He will declare to them all that they have done. (6:108)

It is obvious that God Almighty never guided the Muslims to require others not to abuse Him or the Prophet of Islam; instead, God Almighty advised Muslims to refrain from using derogatory language about the idols of others. That would only provoke them and in return they would abuse God and His Prophet.

This verse sets an example. Muslims must unilaterally uphold ethical standards on this issue. In other words, the Quran points to the reason for conflict: provocation. If one refrains from provocation, one will automatically save oneself from retaliation.

If you are hurt by the negative statements of others, you are not allowed to demand that others should not hurt you. It is your problem and not that of others. According to Quranic teachings, one must keep one's patience and refrain from giving the other party the chance to hit back. This principle can be called the 'save yourself' formula. Don't make demands of others, but rather control yourself in your speech and behaviour.

It is not the believer's job to complain about others' behaviour or to demand that others remain silent or refrain from using such language as does not suit the believers.

This formula gives the easiest solution to problems of antagonism. Moreover, by this method you can save your time and energy and can find more time for constructive activities. This formula saves you from being a victim of distraction, for distraction always leads to useless, time-consuming activities.

It is pointless to say to others: "Don't hurt me!" It is better to avoid hurting others and then the problem is instantly solved. If anyone reviles God or the Prophet, God will punish him, if he has committed a crime in the actual sense of the word. It is not the believer's job to complain about others' behaviour or to demand that others remain silent or refrain from using such language as does not suit the believers. Everyone is accountable before God and God knows how to deal with people's misdemeanours.

How to Avoid Tension

How to attain a tension-free life? It is a question asked by every man and woman. The Quran gives us a simple solution, which is mentioned in the chapter of the Quran entitled *Al-Ra'd* (The Thunder). The relevant Quranic verse is as follows:

> Those who believe and whose hearts find comfort in
> the remembrance of God—surely in the remembrance
> of God hearts can find comfort. (13:28)

This Quranic verse refers to the creation plan of God. The formula given in this verse is:

> Contentment in this world is only for those who
> willingly accept the creation plan of God.

According to the Quranic explanation, the present world was created for only a limited period and also for a temporary purpose—that is, to develop your personality so that you may become eligible to enter the next world that is called Paradise.

Now the problem is that, although man was born with an ideal nature, and is an ideal-seeking animal—in the sense of wanting to have all the best things in life—the present world was not created for this purpose. In terms of personality development, the present world has enormous scope but, in terms of material achievement, the present world is very limited in its scope.

Those who want to fulfil their material desires in the present world will very soon find that they have failed to build the edifice of their dreams. Anything that they achieve seems to them less than ideal. This is a source of all kinds of tension and stress.

The formula given in the Quran is this: try your best to evolve your personality in terms of spiritual development and intellectual development. But, as far as your material requirements are concerned, adopt the need-based formula and not the greed-based formula. All kinds of tension and stress are the result of trying to achieve things that are not achievable in this world.

The problem is that people judge things by a wrong yardstick; they judge their achievements by an ideal yardstick. This is unrealistic. The realistic formula is: use the ideal yardstick only when judging your personality development. But when it comes to your material needs, use a different yardstick. Here, you have to realize that only less than ideal can be achieved.

If you want to have a tension-free life in this world, adopt the realistic approach. Don't run after your desires, for, in reality, they are impossible to fulfil.

No Discrimination

As in other societies of the world, the Arab people were also obsessed with colour and other differences among people. They discriminated against those who were apparently inferior to others. This was not only an Arab phenomenon: it was universal in that age. With this background, God Almighty revealed this verse in the chapter *Al-Hujurat* (The Apartments) of the Quran:

> Mankind! We have created you from a male and female, and made you into peoples and tribes, so that you might come to know each other. The noblest of you in God's sight is the one who fears God most. God is all-knowing and all-aware. (49:13)

According to this verse, the Quran believes in global brotherhood and not just Muslim brotherhood. In fact, in all matters, the Quran adopts a universal rather than any kind of sectarian approach. There are many verses in the Quran that denote that the readers of the Quran are *al-nas* (mankind) and not merely a community.

It is a fact that there are differences between people in terms of colour, etc. But these differences have nothing to do with the superiority or inferiority of different individuals or groups. They are natural differences and they exist for the sole purpose of people being able to recognize each other without any difficulty.

According to the above Quranic verse, the importance of

a person or group will be judged solely on merit. The basis of classification between people is only one and, that is, merit.

Merit-based classification cannot be termed discrimination. It is a sound method of categorizing people. As such, it is a source of motivation and creates an atmosphere of healthy competition. It is a guarantee of social development on a real basis.

Discrimination on the basis of colour, etc., is a negative practice, while classification on the basis of merit promotes love and respect among people. It ensures that no member of society will be denied justice. It creates an atmosphere conducive to development and progress and gives everyone the chance to contribute in a positive way to society. Discrimination creates disunity among people, while following Quranic principles produces unity and harmony among different sections of society. The latter promotes the spirit of mutual respect.

Discrimination on the basis of colour, etc., is a negative practice, while classification on the basis of merit promotes love and respect among people.

According to the Quran and biological research, all men and women have a common ancestor. So, according to this, all men and women are blood sisters and blood brothers to each other. The whole of mankind is a global family.

Waste of Money

There is a general tendency for those who earn money to believe that it is their own property. They feel that they can spend their money as they please without any restrictions from outside. This tendency was also prevalent in Arab society. With this background, the Quran in the chapter *Al-A'raf* (The Heights) gives this general guidance:

> O Children of Adam, dress yourself properly whenever you are at worship: and eat and drink but do not be wasteful: God does not like wasteful people. (7:31)

Spending your money is not simply a matter of choice. There are other aspects to be considered. For example, if, by spending your money you take unhealthy food or unhealthy drink, it will destroy your physical fitness. You will cause your health and your activities in life to deteriorate.

Money is a great source of distraction, and it is this distraction that is called in the Quran 'israf'. Israf literally means going beyond all limits.

In fact, money has two different aspects—the positive and the negative. Positive expenditure of money is undoubtedly good but negative expenditure of money is bad.

Money is a great source of distraction, and it is this distraction that is called in the Quran 'israf'. Israf literally means going beyond all limits. And, in this sense, any waste of money is israf. When one indulges in israf, it will very soon become a habit and one will habitually go beyond limits in other matters also. And that will prove to be disastrous.

Money is a great asset for the earner. It helps him to live a better life. It helps to pay the bills for his real needs. But when he fails to differentiate between positive expenditure and negative expenditure, it shows that he has become the slave of his desires, spending his money on such items as afford no real benefit in life.

For this reason, every man and woman must be very cautious in his or her shopping, buying in a strictly selective way. When you are in a shopping centre, don't give in to whims of the moment, but see what your real needs are. The system of modern shopping, or modern consumerism, is the greatest cause of the wastage of money.

Use your money on things that give you some constructive result in return. The kind of expenditure that is not going to give you any return is a sheer waste of money. Spending money is like sowing a seed. If the seed will bring you a good harvest, then it is well worth sowing, otherwise better not sow it at all. The same is true of spending money.

Setting a Tradition

In the earliest days of the human race, Adam and Eve, who founded the first generation, had two sons, Cain and Abel. For no good reason, the elder brother, Cain, became angry and killed his younger brother, Abel. This was a very serious crime, after which God sent His guidance to the prophet of that time. This divine guidance is quoted thus in the Quran:

> That was why We laid it down for the Children of Israel that whoever killed a human being—except as a punishment for murder or for spreading corruption in the land—shall be regarded as having killed all mankind, and that whoever saved a human life shall be regarded as having saved all mankind. (5:32)

Why does God Almighty say that killing a person is like killing all mankind, and giving life to a person is like giving life to all mankind? This question underlines the importance of tradition.

As the saying goes, 'It requires a lot of history to make a little tradition'. This means that if you want to establish a good tradition in society, you need several precedents to make it a social norm; moreover, if you have established a wrong tradition in society, it again needs a long process of change to abolish this wrong tradition and replace it with a healthy tradition.

A society does not abide by laws but by traditions. Laws have a very limited role in social reform. The same is true of the family. Both behave strictly according to traditions and not in obedience to any kind of laws. Therefore, in the case of the family and also in the case of a society—even in the case of a nation, one must be very prudent in this regard.

One example of the lack of prudence is the fostering of the present concept of freedom. In present times, people generally take freedom as the *summum bonum*, or the greatest good. This modern concept of freedom has broken all those traditions that have been a part of every society for the past thousands and thousands of years.

For example, whereas the ancient societies were based on the concept of human duties, the present concept of freedom has wiped out the former concept of human duties, replacing it with an overemphasis on human rights. For this reason, we see that everywhere people are rights-conscious rather than duty-conscious. The entire fabric of society has been upset by this change.

Be very cautious, therefore, about tampering with those traditions which relate both to the family and to society.

Anger Management

Social problems are the constant concern of the Quran and it sets about addressing them. One of these kinds of problems is anger—a phenomenon which is in evidence in every society. In fact, wherever there are two persons, there must also be provocation and anger. On this subject, the Quran gives a piece of guidance in the chapter *Al-'Imran* (The Family of Imran). Its translation is as follows:

> For those who spend, both in prosperity and adversity, who restrain their anger and are forgiving towards their fellow men—God loves those who do good works. (3:134)

In this verse the Quran does not say that a true believer is devoid of anger; it says instead that a true believer is one who is able to restrain his anger. So, the definition of a true believer is not one who is free of anger, but one whose faith is so powerful that he is able to control his temper whenever the fire of anger begins to smoulder in his heart.

Anger is a negative reaction. But a true believer is one who has the ability to give a positive response at that time.

Anger is not an evil. It is a part of human nature. In fact, anger is a negative expression of a healthy aspect of human nature. Man is a sensitive animal endowed with intuition and, by his intuition, he knows what is good and what is bad. So, it is but natural that when he sees some unprincipled behaviour or an immoral act, he becomes disturbed. But in such a situation, there are two options: to show a negative reaction or give a positive response.

Anger is a negative reaction. But a true believer is one who has the ability to give a positive response at that time. A negative response arises out of hate, whereas a positive response flows from love and compassion. A true believer must develop compassion in that situation. He must try to reform his bad habits. He must try to de-condition his conditioning. The message of the Quranic verse is: Do not give a hateful reaction but try rather to give a compassionate response.

Anger is generally the result of provocation and provocation is a test of your capacity to exercise self-control. It helps to view provocation simply as a challenge to your imperturbability. So at the time of provocation, prove to be a person who can maintain his equilibrium and rise above all irritants. Be the master of your negative sentiments. This upholds the true dignity of human beings, both men and women.

Hopeful Beginning

Bismillah hir rehman ir rahim is the first verse of the Quran. It is repeated no less than one hundred and fourteen times. This repetition shows that, according to the Quran, this verse has great importance in the scheme of things given in the Quran.

The translation of this verse is: "In the name of God, the Most Gracious, the Most Merciful." The Prophet of Islam said that at the beginning of everything you do you should recite this verse. So, one can say that this is the word of beginning.

Beginning in this way is very important. It gives you great hope.

After reciting this, you can believe that you are starting your work in a world that is controlled by God Almighty and that, if you follow the right path, you will have divine help bestowed upon you.

This belief, freeing you of tension and despair, gives you great psychological courage. It inculcates the spirit of positivity. The recitation of this verse is not simply lip-service: it shows your conviction about the creation plan of God.

Recitation of this word not only gives you courage but it also helps you to build a positive mode in your personality. This positivity makes you able to plan your life on a realistic basis. This removes all the negative thoughts from your mind. It enhances your creativity.

Saying Bismillah is, thus, an acknowledgement of the higher authority—that without God's blessings you could not achieve anything in this world.

When you say, "I begin in the name of God Almighty," you establish a relationship with the greatest power of the universe. You feel that you are not alone in this world. God Almighty is on your side. You feel that you are not an alien in this world, but an integral part of your surroundings.

Saying *bismillah hir rahman ir rahim* is not a ritual. It is a real part of belief. It is a conscious act. On the one hand, it is an acknowledgement of the Creator of the Universe and, on the other, it is a solemn expression of honesty and sincerity.

'I begin in the name of God' means I ask for the help of God Almighty in my work and in my life. Reciting these words amounts to refining your soul and engineering your mind on the lines of modesty. It is an acknowledgement from the creature to the Creator. Saying *Bismillah* is, thus, an acknowledgement of the higher authority—that without God's blessings you could not achieve anything in this world.

In the chapter *Al-Qalam* (the Pen), the Quran narrates the story of certain horticulturalists who omitted to say *Bismillah*. This event is referred to in the Quran as follows:

> We have tried them as we tried the owners of a certain orchard, who vowed to harvest all its fruits the next morning, without saying, 'If it be God's will.' A calamity from your Lord befell the orchard as they slept. And by morning it lay as if it had already been harvested. (68:17- 20)

This means that no one can achieve anything in this world without it being God's will. God is the Lord of this universe. When one says *Bismillah*, one invokes God to provide His help. This is like seeking the permission of God Almighty. So, saying *Bismillah* ensures the success of any task in this world.

Peace of Mind

Everyone has a mind but peace of mind is a rare phenomenon. Everyone wants to live in peace but peace eludes almost everyone. Perhaps it is the greatest problem of the human world. What is the solution to this problem?

The Quran gives a solution to this problem in unequivocal terms. It is recorded in the chapter *Al-Ra'd* (Thunder):

> Those who believe and whose hearts find comfort in the remembrance of God—surely in the remembrance of God hearts can find comfort. (13:28)

Here 'remembrance of God' does not mean that simply reciting the word 'God' (Allah) can give you peace of mind. It means that, in reality, contentment is only for those who accept the creation plan of God.

More particularly, this means that this world having been created by God and God having laid down all the laws of nature, anyone who wants to live with a peaceful mind in this world must know the creation plan of God and try to live in accordance with it.

According to this divine plan, man was created as an ideal-seeking animal. Everyone is therefore an idealist by birth. But the present world is not an ideal world. Man's mind may in its capacity be unlimited, but our world is one of limitations. It is this contradiction between the two that creates problems. Tension of mind is a result of the gap between seeker and achievement.

Fulfilment of all desires cannot be a goal for a person in this world. You should learn the art of desire management rather than try to fulfil all your desires.

No one can alter the course of divine creation. In this situation you have only one option and that is to adjust yourself to the external world, rather than try to mould the world according to your own desires.

Fulfilment of all desires cannot be a goal for a person in this world. You should learn the art of desire management rather than try to fulfil all your desires. But here is good news for every man and woman: although the material world is limited, the world of thought is unlimited.

We must set our goals in life in terms of intellectual achievement and not in terms of material achievement. The intellectual world is so vast that there is no end to intellectual activity. The intellectual journey can go beyond space and time, while material activities cannot.

The present situation is a blessing from God. It is God's

will that man should adopt the principle of contentment as regards material things. But as far as intellectual achievement is concerned, there is no limit at all. God Almighty wants to see every man and woman as a super achiever—but in terms of intellectual goals and not in terms of material goals.

If you travel westward across the Atlantic and start your journey from the African coast, the American coast will be the limit. But if you try to discover the laws of the universe, then there is no limit. The world of facts has no limits, so you can continue your journey in it forever.

If you want to have a peaceful mind, adopt the formula—simple living, high thinking.

Mission and Profession

The Book of God is a book of guidance. It gives people the kind of guidelines that make them able to receive the blessings of God when they follow them in letter and spirit. But in the latter days the divine book has become the central symbol of a religious community. With this second phase, a new dimension has been added to the divine book, that is, the commercial factor.

For the generation of latter times, the Book of God has become a source of pride—a kind of market commodity, an easy device by which to secure the respect of others. In the first period the Book of God was strictly a book of guidance but, in the later period, it became a book of material interest.

Taking the Book of God in its first sense then is a mission. It means that you do not attach any material interest to the Book of God and do not want to derive any commercial benefit from it. You have involved yourself with the divine book for the sake of God and not for the sake of anything else. This kind of involvement with the Book of God is a mission. It will bring you great reward from God Almighty.

But if your main concern is your own agenda, you have not studied the book sincerely to find out what the Quran really requires, and are simply following what is in your mind and doing so in the name of the Book of God, then it is a profession. It is like commercializing the Book of God. It is like making the divine book a trading commodity rather than taking it as a source of true guidance.

The Book of God is a book of guidance. It gives people the kind of guidelines that make them able to receive the blessings of God when they follow them in letter and spirit.

It is this latter use of the Book of God that is mentioned in the chapter Al-'Imran (The Family of Imran) with reference to the children of Israel. It is also applicable to the Muslim community. The translation of these verses is as follows:

> God made a covenant with those who were given the Book to make it known to people and not conceal it. But they cast it behind their backs and bartered it for a paltry price: what an evil bargain they made! Those who exult in their misdeeds and love to be praised for what they have not done should not suppose that they are secure from punishment; they shall suffer a grievous punishment. (3:187-188)

This Quranic verse mentions that kind of practice when a community takes the Quran as its profession rather than as its mission, when it tries to secure material benefits from the Book of God, not only in monetary terms but also in terms of fame, popularity, leadership, image building, etc.

This kind of behaviour—a profession rather than a true mission—is not acceptable to God. It is like taking credit for a deed that one has not done. Professionalization of the Quran is no better than totally abandoning it.

The Value of Silence

One of the values on which the Quran lays emphasis is silence. But it is not silence just for the sake of silence. Quranic silence is for contemplation, to understand more and more, to enhance your learning. It is a culture of silence in the complete sense of the word. There is a relevant verse in the chapter Al-A'raf (The Heights), the translation of which is as follows:

When the Quran is read, listen to it with attention, and hold your peace, so that you may receive mercy. (7:204)

This means that when the Quran is recited, you should remain silent and listen to it with total attention. This verse gives us a general principle with a particular reference, that is, when you read or listen to or observe something, keep complete silence and try to understand it, focusing all your attention on it. This kind of habit is very important if the spirit of learning is to be inculcated.

The Quran tries to develop one's thinking capacity, it tries to build a mind that can understand things in their deeper sense and analyze them with objectivity. The art of silence is necessary to be able to accomplish all these things.

There is a saying: "When I am speaking, I am not listening,

and when I am not listening, I am not learning." This saying has the same meaning as is expressed in the aforementioned verse of the Quran.

Silence is not simply refraining from speech. It is more than that. When the human mind, with its unlimited capacity, stops speaking, it instantly starts thinking. The mind is a super computer, switched on at the time of birth and continuing to function eternally. It can never be switched off. Thinking is a continuous process of the mind. The word 'rest' is not to be found in the human lexicon where the mind is concerned.

What is thinking? It is to reflect, it is to consider, it is to activate and utilize your intellectual capacity. Bringing the intellectual faculties into play enables one to arrive at meaningful conclusions. The mind is the most elevated part of a human being and thinking is its supreme role.

The Quran tries to develop one's thinking capacity, it tries to build a mind that can understand things in their deeper sense and analyze them with objectivity.

It is said that man is a thinking animal. So thinking is the most important process which occurs in a human being. All the great discoveries have been the result of thinking.

But thinking is not an occasional activity of the mind: it is a continuous process, and it happens not only in the daytime, but also when you are asleep at night. The only difference at that time is that it is transferred from the conscious to the subconscious mind.

The issue of silence can be understood in this context. According to the nature of mind, speaking means to stop the process of thinking, while when you are silent you are allowing your mind to carry on its thinking processes without any interruption. Just as a speed breaker on the road reduces the speed of the passing vehicles, human speech breaks man's continuous journey of thought. Silence is a positive habit, it helps you to learn more and more and develop your personality unhindered.

Right Use of Speech

People are generally in the habit of speaking more and thinking less. The Quran is critical of this unhealthy habit. In the chapter *Al-Nisa'* (Women), the Quran says:

> There is no good in most of their secret talk, except in the case of those who enjoin charity and kindness, or reconciliation between people. If anyone does that, seeking the pleasure of God, We will give him an immense reward. (4:114)

This Quranic verse sets the standard for secret as well as open talk, namely, soundness and utility. One can only live up to this standard by being sincere in what one says and speaking only after analyzing the matter in hand. What one says should stem from a positive mind. According to this verse, a person must refrain from futile talk. He should never indulge in talking just for the sake of talking.

Now, the question is, what is the best manner of speaking? And what content of one's speech may be regarded as worthwhile? The Quranic criterion for proper social intercourse is based on three principles. All three principles are described in the above verse of the Quran, which sets them forth as follows:

1. Charity, that is, speaking with the true giving spirit;

2. Kindness, that is, speaking with the spirit of well-wishing towards others;

3. Conciliation, that is, speaking in such a way as to create an atmosphere of harmony among people.

This is what constitutes well thought-out speech and is the only legitimate use of one's tongue. This kind of speech is useful to both the speaker as well as the listener. For the speaker's part, it conveys sincerity and positivity, while for the listener it is also fruitful in all respects.

The tongue is a very important organ of a human being; but it is like a double-edged sword. It has plus points as well as minus points. The right use of the tongue can produce a healthy atmosphere in society. Conversely, the wrong use of the tongue is so baneful that it may destroy the whole social fabric. The right use of the tongue can create the spirit of love among people, while the wrong use of the tongue will create hatred and intolerance in society.

The tongue is a very important organ of a human being; but it is like a double-edged sword. It has plus points as well as minus points.

The tongue is a great blessing for mankind. No creature other than man possesses such an asset. Meaningful speech is a very rare phenomenon in the universe. No two astronomical bodies, no two trees, no two animals, and no mountain or river can enter into a meaningful conversation. It is only human beings who have this unique capacity.

But in terms of use, this unique blessing can be described in two different ways—healthy use and unhealthy use. One who uses his tongue along healthy lines will receive a double reward. This will help develop his personality and then he will receive more and more blessings from the Creator. Make your speech the result of positive thinking, rather than an abrupt expression of ill-considered ideas.

The Complex-free Soul

In the chapter *Al-Fajr* (The Dawn) the Quran states that the reality of human life is coloured by human responses to it. One who responds to situations negatively is a failure, whereas one who responds to situations positively is a success. After explaining this, the Quran says:

> [But to the righteous, God will say], 'O soul at peace, return to your Lord, well-pleased, well-pleasing. Join My servants. Enter My Paradise.' (89:27-30)

According to this, the best course for man to take is to prove that he is a complex-free soul. A complex-free soul is one who accepts the creation plan of God, who can give a positive response in any situation, good or bad, who develops no negative feelings in any adverse situation and who never becomes proud or arrogant in a favourable situation. He is one who can face either situation with a balanced attitude. He is the one who stands up to the test.

Our world is a world of differences, unwanted situations and provocations, therefore, at all times we have to face predicaments that are not to our liking. This diversity of situation is a part of nature. Since no one can remedy this, one cannot a world free of all these aspects. We have no option but to accept the world as it is.

Man is required to face all these odds with a tranquil mind. He is required to take them as a challenge and to do so in a positive way. Man is required to give a positive response even in negative situations. Those who prove themselves capable of doing this are complex-free souls.

A complex-free soul is one who accepts God's scheme: in return God will accept him and reward him with eternal Paradise. A complex-free soul does not mean a soul without complexes. A complex-free soul is one who is able to deal with all kind of adversity. A complex-free soul exhibits the capacity to manage things rather than the capacity to eliminate them.

The 'management of odds' is not simply the management of unwanted situations. It is more than that. There are always untoward factors in the external world but the art of their management is a function of the mind. It is the mind that, by its internal exercises, can manage all external factors.

This means that all those external problems have their plus points. That is, they can serve as food for the mind, but only if you prove to have that kind of mind which has developed the art of difference management.

A complex-free soul is one who accepts God's scheme: in return God will accept him and reward him with eternal Paradise.

A prejudiced mind is the opposite of the complex-free soul. Manage the intellectual problems, make yourself free of all kinds of prejudices and then you will become a complex-free soul. A complex-free soul is the highest state according to Quranic ethics and the way to achieve this elevated state is to keep your mind positive at all costs.

The Art of Acceptance

here are a number of verses in the Quran that emphasize the importance of patience (*sabr*) and tolerance (*eraz*). One verse says that those who are patient will be granted the greatest reward (39:10). If you read the Quran, you will find that almost all its commandments are based, directly or indirectly, on this spirit.

Why has such great importance been attached to patience? It is certainly not a virtue which stems from passivity. And there is great wisdom behind this teaching for it shows a realistic approach. It is, in essence, the art of acceptance. It means that you should accept others so that they will accept you too.

When we travel on the road, we always follow a well-known traffic principle: Stick to your lane. This kind of traffic rule is based on mutual acceptance; it means that you should follow your own lane and I should follow my lane and this will allow room for both.

The same is required in our entire social life, for social life is like living in a crowd. If you want to go ahead, you have to make room for others; this is the most important principle for a successful social life. If you want to give a new name to this culture, you could call it the art of acceptance or the culture of acceptance.

The art of acceptance means the art of difference management or the art of peaceful adjustment. All these expressions are quite synonymous with each other. By adopting the art of acceptance, you give respect to others. It is like proceeding to your destination without hindering anyone else.

God created man and He granted freedom to every man and woman. In terms of freedom there is no difference between people, so everyone tries to exercise his freedom. This may create conflict between different groups. The above teaching gives us a practical formula by which to run our society smoothly: the art of acceptance.

Acceptance is not simply a matter of adjustment. It also has great wisdom. When you follow the culture of acceptance, you foster many good values in your personality, for example, positive thinking, giving respect to others, establishing your dignity, impacting upon others as a mature person, showing that you are a person of high thinking. Then you prove that you are free of tension, free of hate, free of intolerance, free of negativity, and so on.

The art of acceptance means the art of difference management or the art of peaceful adjustment.

The art of acceptance is the art of development in terms of spirituality and in terms of thinking. When you accept others, you save yourself from distraction. When you accept others, you invite them to open up opportunities for you. When you accept others, it is a silent request to them to do the same as done by you.

The art of acceptance is intimately related to the art of living. Successful living in this world is not possible unless this formula is followed. In short, accept others and others will be compelled to accept you.

Spiritual Partners

~§§§~

The Quran gives great importance to the institution of marriage. According to the Quran, the home is the first unit of any society, and is the primary source of all kinds of valuable experiences. If the home is good, then the whole of society will automatically emerge as a good society.

In the Quran, there are several verses to this effect, covering different aspects of the institution of marriage. In the chapter *Al-Rum* (The Romans), the Quran gives basic guidelines in this regard. The translation of one of these verses is as follows:

> Another of His signs is that He created for you from among yourselves spouses, so that you might find repose in them, and He created between you affection and kindness. Truly there are signs in this for people who reflect. (30:21)

In these verses, the Quran reveals an important law of nature, that is, that a man and a woman are the counterparts of each other. According to a saying of the Prophet, men and women are two equal halves of a single unit. A man and a woman as a pair can fulfil the real purpose of human life.

According to this, man and woman are spiritual partners to each other. Mutual love and affection are the binding forces for both. Starting life as a pair enables them to have experiences of an elevated nature. In their daily meetings, they can share spiritual experiences and through discussion they can plan their lives on a spiritual basis. They can find time for joint study. They can together embark on discovering broader areas of the spiritual world.

Man and woman are born partners to each other. This natural pair has the enormous capacity to develop their personalities in terms of spirituality. The combination of a man and a woman gives both of them great opportunities to unfold the hidden treasure of spirituality in their nature. Both men and women are like cogwheels. One cog cannot move the wheel: the wheel of life can be moved only with the joint effort of both.

But there is a price to be paid for this. Without paying this price, no pair can move the wheel of life. This price, in a single word, is none other than adjustment. The fact is that in spite of all their similarities, both have been born with differences. Difference is a part of nature. There is no uniformity in the scheme of things in nature. So, we have no option but to learn the art of difference management.

Man and woman are spiritual partners to each other. Mutual love and affection are the binding forces for both.

One's failure in this regard is tantamount to failure in life itself. If you want to develop your spirituality, try to adjust with your spouse. Spirituality is the highest goal one can aim to achieve. Without spirituality, man and woman are both incomplete. Spirituality gives you wisdom and strength. And both are necessary to have a successful life.

Spirituality leads to personality development. And only developed personalities can attain the status of super achievers in this world.

De-condition the Mind

The chapter *Al-Shams* (The Sun) of the Quran sets forth a very important principle, termed in modern language the principle of de-conditioning. The translation of the relevant verses is as follows:

> He who purifies it will indeed be successful, and he who pollutes it is sure to fail. (91:9-10)

In this Quranic verse, to 'pollute' means 'conditioning' and to 'purify' means 'de-conditioning'. According to this, everyone is born as Mr. Nature, but due to environmental influences, he deviates from his original nature and becomes Mr. Conditioned. The first need for every man and woman is to make himself or herself again Mr. or Ms. Nature. If he or she is to revert to his or her original nature, it requires de-conditioning of the conditioned mind. This de-conditioning is imperative if objective thinking is to be evolved. Conditioning makes one a biased person, whereas de-conditioning brings one back to one's true nature, so that one again becomes Mr. Nature.

There is no other way to develop your potential other than de-conditioning or cleansing.

In the physical world, an onion is an example of this psychological process. Every onion has a core but this core is covered over by many layers. If you peel off these layers down to the last one, you will reach the core, and the same is true of most men and women. Their personalities are layered over by different kind of biases and prejudices. It is only de-conditioning that will

84

remove these external forms of pollution and restore the human personality to its pristine state.

In this sense, one can say that every human being has two different periods of his life—the pre-maturity period and the post-maturity period. In the former period, due to conditioning, everyone's mind is full of different elements, both black and white. Thus everyone's mind is a jungle of thoughts. De-conditioning then basically calls for the mind to be sorted out. Through introspection or self-criticism, all those notions which are really undesirable can be discovered. The fact is that in the age of immaturity, no one has the power to distinguish between the true and the specious, so he imbibes everything indiscriminately. Now he needs to cast out all erroneous and therefore superfluous ideas. For this, he has to develop the power to recognize which are the undesirable elements of which he must rid his mind, so as to make himself a purified person or a de-conditioned mind.

There is no mathematical way to sort out this mixture of good and bad. It is a completely subjective process. Everyone must develop the power to distinguish between wanted and unwanted things, between biased and unbiased opinions. This kind of ability is a must if you are to de-condition your conditioning.

Why de-condition? The process of conditioning has a deleterious effect upon your personality. It is the art of de-conditioning that makes you able to return to your original status. The process of de-conditioning is a process of cleansing. There is no other way to develop your potential other than de-conditioning or cleansing.

De-conditioning is not a very easy process. You have to initiate a relentless process by which to identify and eliminate all undesirable facets of your personality. It is like self-flagellation, during which you should be prepared to accept all kinds of criticism. Conditioning is like living in darkness, whereas de-conditioning means re-entering the golden light of day.

Negative Remarks

*I*n the chapter *Al-Hujurat* (The Apartments), the Quran gives a commandment relating to social ethics. The translation of this verse is as follows:

> Believers, let not some men among you ridicule others: it may be that the latter are better than the former: nor should some women laugh at others: it may be that the latter are better than the former: do not defame or be sarcastic to each other, or call each other by [offensive] nicknames. How bad it is to earn an evil reputation after accepting the faith! Those who do not repent are evil-doers. (49:11)

Those negative habits referred to in this verse relate to the use of the tongue. People generally tend to point out others' weaknesses and, even if there are none, they will try to invent some, and then make negative remarks.

Giving people nicknames or making derogatory remarks is a common habit in both men and women. Giving a nickname means calling someone by the wrong name. This kind of negative remark worsens the healthy atmosphere of a society. It is like social pollution. Believers are strongly exhorted not to indulge in such negative practices.

Making negative remarks about others is not simply bad for others, but acts like a boomerang. It is bad for both the parties. A person who uses such undesirable language pollutes his own nature, having committed a moral crime by uttering negative words against another. Moreover, he pollutes the ethical atmosphere of the whole of society.

This is a general piece of advice, but it is meant especially for believers, because believers are those who have given a firm commitment to God Almighty, in terms of which they are not supposed to indulge in this kind of unworthy activity. This is tantamount to breaking the solemn pledge they have taken at the time of declaring their belief.

It is a fact that to err is human. Nevertheless, if anyone indulges in these unwanted practices, even if it is unintentionally or mistakenly, he must, on the one hand, apologize to the person about whom he has passed a negative remark, and, on the other hand, he should ask for forgiveness from God Almighty. Repentance is as good as correcting your mistake.

Every man and woman is responsible for building a healthy society. It is their social duty not to indulge in such activities as may cause damage to the healthy atmosphere of a society.

The individual has only two options: either he should refrain from indulging in such undesirable activities or, even if he only occasionally commits this kind of error, he must very soon repent and try, in all sincerity, to compensate for it by taking corrective measures.

Every man and woman is responsible for building a healthy society. It is their social duty not to indulge in such activities as may cause damage to the healthy atmosphere of a society. These kinds of practices are against the plan made by the Creator. Calling others by nicknames, passing derogatory remarks, or attempting character assassination, are all like poison, not in the physical sense, but in the psychological or ethical sense. Believers are required to be self-disciplined in their morality, for those who fail to adopt this kind of ethical discipline will be severely punished by God.

Conspiracy: Not a Problem

eople commonly think in terms of conspiracy. Both men and women are frequently obsessed by this notion. The result is that people are living with a kind of besieged mentality. The Quran wants to put an end to this kind of negative mentality. In the chapter *Al-'Imran* (The Family of Imran), the Quran gives us a very important piece of guidance on this subject. The translation of the relevant verse is as follows:

> Whenever something good happens to you, it grieves them; but when evil befalls you, they rejoice. If you persevere and fear God, their conspiracies will never harm you in the least: God encompasses all that they do. (3:120)

This Quranic verse reveals a law of nature. It is a universal law and it is applicable everywhere and at all times. Everyone can follow this advice and solve the problem of conspiracy.

According to this Quranic verse, the existence of a conspiracy is not the problem. It is a lack of patience and sincerity which is the real problem. Patience means not to react immediately to a situation but to give a well-considered response to the problem.

Our world is a world of competition. Moreover, everyone is free to do what one wants to do. In such a situation it is not possible to have a world that is completely free of conspiracies. You cannot eliminate the phenomenon of conspiracy or bad designs, but it is certainly possible to save yourself from being a victim of its harm. And the formula is very simple: By keeping patience and being sincere, you can make the conspiracy ineffective for you.

The best defence of conspiracy or bad design is to take it as a challenge rather than as a manifestation of enmity. Exert your energy on only one front, that is, to meet the challenge. This is the best way to cope with the problem of conspiracy.

Conspiracy or bad design is not an evil. It has great positive value. In fact it serves as a blessing in disguise. It shocks your mind and activates your intellect. It helps to turn your potential into actuality. It saves you from being a victim of stagnation.

Give positive response to a situation. Assess the situation dispassionately. Plan your action with an objective mind.

Conspiracy is a phenomenon of competition and not a phenomenon of enmity. In this world of competition, everyone is practically a 'conspirator'. Others are engaged in conspiracies against you and you also are engaged in conspiracies against others, sometimes consciously and sometimes unconsciously, sometimes directly and sometimes indirectly. Conspiracy is not a monopoly of others. No one in this world is free from this practice. There is only one place that is free from conspiracy or bad design and that is the graveyard.

So, take it easy. Don't waste your time in complaint and protest. Give positive response to a situation. Assess the situation dispassionately. Plan your action with an objective mind.

By applying wisdom, manage your emotions. Face the situation with a normal mind. Try to win over your self and you will be able to win the whole world of conspiracy and enmity.

The secret of success and failure both can be summed up in these words: the result of negative response is failure, and the result of positive response is success.

The Best Way of Settlement

*he Quran points out that the whole material world is a world of peace. Stars are constantly moving, but there is no clash whatsoever between them. According to the Quranic scheme, the same world culture is required of mankind also. In the chapter *Al-Nisa'* (Women) the Quran gives guidelines on this subject. The translation of the relevant verse is as follows:

> If a woman fears ill-treatment or indifference on the part of her husband, it shall be no offence for her to seek a reconciliation, for reconciliation is best. But people are prone to selfish greed. If you do good and fear Him, surely God is aware of what you do. (4:128)

Here, the Quran enjoins us to adopt the policy of reconciliation in controversial matters. The immediate context of this verse is the resolution of husband-wife differences, but the Quran, by giving a particular reference, gives a general direction. The policy of reconciliation is not only effective for problems between husband and wife, but is equally useful for all other problems, both national and international.

When controversy arises, reconciliation is the best course. That is, you have to adopt a conciliatory rather than a confrontational approach. The conciliatory approach always minimizes the problem, while the confrontational approach aggravates matters, while leaving the initial problem unsolved.

The fact is that you are not living on an isolated island; you are bound to live in society. You have no option other than to live with others, with a family, with a society, with a nation—this list goes on to international affairs. In such a situation, you cannot afford to live on your own. If you become egocentric and ignore other people, you will unnecessarily make others your rivals, so the best policy is to accept others, adopting the policy of adjustment. You have to avoid all kinds of clash, so that you may save your energy and your time.

Adopting the policy of reconciliation is not just a question of being accommodating towards others. It is much more than that. It allows you to continue your journey of life without any break. It saves you from deviation and permits you to dedicate your life more and more to worthy goals.

If you adopt the policy of confrontation, you will very soon discover that there is no end to your difficulties. Arising out of differences, it leads to clashes and clashes will culminate in violence. And, of course, the next stage after violence is war and fighting. The best policy, therefore, is to rid oneself of the confrontational mentality at the very outset.

Adopting the policy of reconciliation is not just a question of being accommodating towards others. It allows you to continue your journey of life without any break.

Conciliatory approach seems to be directed against another person, but in fact the confrontational approach is against the law of nature. It is a man-versus-nature issue rather than a man-versus-man issue. You cannot change the course of nature, so there is no option other than to seek settlement with nature. This is the only way of success in this world.

Sound Speech

$\mathcal{T}$ he Quran greatly emphasizes on sound speech or straight speech. This is very important in social life. In the chapter

Al-Ahzab (The Confederates) the Quran gives its guidance in this regard in these words:

> Believers, fear God, and say the straight speech. He will make your conduct sound and forgive you your sins. Whoever obeys God and His Messenger has indeed achieved a great success. (33:70-71)

The fear of God is not simply a fear, fear of God makes you highly sincere, it makes you responsible, it makes you honest, and it is these qualities that make you able to speak in a sound manner. And there is no doubt about it that sound thinking has the greatest importance in terms of personality development as well as in terms of building a better society.

Sound thinking leads to sound speech. Sound speech is one in which there is no confusion and which is based on facts. Sound thinking inculcates realistic thinking and it is realistic approach that leads to all kinds of success.

Sound speech or sound writing represents the whole personality of a man. Sound speech or sound writing is a sign of an integrated personality.

Sound speech or sound writing is easily understandable. It addresses peoples mind, it touches the heart of men and women. A sound thinker always speaks in the language of nature, and nature is common to both the speaker and the listener. It is this commonality that makes speaking and writing of a sound thinker acceptable to all.

Sound thinking is always based on reason; sound thinking is a result of awakening your mind; sound thinking is an outcome of deep contemplation; sound thinking is free of all kinds of bias and prejudice.

Due to this quality sound speech and sound writing reaches directly to the heart of the people. It has the power to change people's character. It may revolutionize people's mind. It is this quality of sound speech that can bring about reform in a society. It has the power to build a healthier nation.

Sound speech or sound writing represents the whole personality of a man. Sound speech or sound writing is a sign of an integrated personality. It tells that the concerned person is an honest person. It means that what he is saying is not simply as lip-service on his behalf, but is his sincere opinion. He is free of hypocrisy. There is no difference between his thinking and his speaking.

A person having these qualities is a great asset for his society. His sound thinking is a guarantee that he will not create problems for his fellow beings. He will live as a trustworthy person. He will be free of the self-centred mentality. He will follow his conscience rather than his own interest. He will adopt a principled character. His sound thinking will make him sound in every aspect of life.

According to the Quran, sound speech or right speech is divine speech; it is like speaking the language of Paradise. Paradise is the place where only right persons will find entry, so one who follows this principle, he is liable to seek double blessing by God. He becomes a good member of a society in this world and in the Hereafter he will be accepted as a fortunate member of the society of Paradise.

Universal Brotherhood

*I*n the very first chapter of the Quran, *Al-Fatihah* (The Opening), the concept of universal brotherhood is highlighted. The translation of the relevant verse is as follows:

> All praise is due to God, the Lord of the Universe. (1:2)

According to this Quranic verse, God is not the God of some community or group, He is the God of all mankind. He alone is the Creator; He alone is the Sustainer; He alone is the Lord of the Universe.

This oneness of God is the basis of the oneness of humanity. It means that God is one and so also is humanity. In the eyes of God, there is no difference between one man and another, between the whites and the blacks, between the poor and the rich. When, in the eyes of God, all humanity is one, it is but natural that mankind should adopt this kind of thinking and live as one divine people.

According to this Quranic verse, God is not the God of some community or group, He is the God of all mankind.

There is a beautiful story about the Prophet of Islam which is a fine illustration of this Quranic concept. This story is totally authentic because it is narrated by al-Bukhari, who has the highest status among the group of *muhaddissin* (narrators of the Prophet's traditions). The story goes like this:

> The Prophet of Islam started his mission in 610 AD. Thirteen years later, he migrated to Madinah, the second most important city of Arabia. At that time there were some Jewish tribes living in Madinah. It happened that one day the Prophet saw a funeral procession passing through a street in the town. The Prophet was seated at that time, but on seeing the funeral, he stood up out of respect. Then one of his companions said: "O Prophet, that was the funeral of a Jew. Why are you giving so much respect to a deceased non-Muslim?" The Prophet replied: *Alaysat*

nafsan (Was he not a human being?) (*Sahih al-Bukhari*, 1312)

This example set by the Prophet of Islam shows that irrespective of religion or tradition, all men and women are equal, all are human beings, all are equally honourable members of humanity at large. Everyone was created by God like oneself and one's community. This concept of universality is the first basis of universal unity among all mankind.

Universal brotherhood is not simply an abstract idea. It has the capacity to inculcate the highest human values among all men and women. It widens the horizon of the individual, it makes people broadminded. It elevates people above all kinds of superficial thinking. It gives people a higher standard by which to live their lives. It revolutionizes people's minds and fosters this universal belief: I am for all and all are for me.

The concept of universal brotherhood is a killer of all kinds of negative thinking. It originates a new kind of thinking, by which people are bound to adopt God-based thinking. After adopting this principle, every society becomes a kind of universal society. This concept serves as a bulldozer of all kinds of prejudices and discrimination.

Man and Nature

*I*n the chapter *Al-Kahf* (The Cave), the Quran gives a very important piece of guidance. Addressing the Prophet, the Quran says:

> Keep yourself attached to those who call on their Lord, morning and evening, seeking His pleasure; and do not let your eyes turn away from them, desiring the

attraction of worldly life; and do not obey one whose heart We have made heedless of Our remembrance, one who pursues his own whims and becomes dissolute. (18:28)

This Quranic verse not only sets forth a religious injunction, but it also alludes to a universal law of nature. In one sense, the Quran is a statement of the Laws of Nature. Those who obey these Laws of Nature are successful, while those who try to follow their own whims or desires will be doomed to failure.

Everyone is full of desires. If you simply follow your desires, you will certainly deviate from the right path laid down by God. Those, on the other hand, who control their desires, making every effort to know God's laws as demonstrated in Nature and literally stated in the Quran, have adopted the right path and, sooner or later, they will reach their destination. There are boundaries in every field of life. One should be very serious about this, and should give due respect to these boundaries.

For example, the individual may enjoy his freedom but he should not choose to be an anarchist. He should always follow the peaceful path and never opt for violence He should promote the culture of love in society and not the culture of hate and intolerance; he should speak the truth and never tell a lie. No excuse is acceptable in this matter.

In this world there are two paths to follow: that of one's own whims and that of divine laws. It is obviously easy to obey your whims or to follow your desires. But in the end, this is a disastrous choice. This world was not created by you, but by God Almighty. So you have to adjust yourself to the divine laws. In this world you are free, but your freedom has to have some limitations, and that is to avoid anarchy and adhere to the laws of nature laid down by God. Your freedom should be a disciplined freedom and not unlimited freedom.

The other way is to discover the Laws of Nature and apply

these laws to your life. The Quran is only a literal statement of those laws hidden in nature. If one is sincere, one will discover these laws without fail.

Those, who control their desires, making every effort to know God's laws as demonstrated in Nature and literally stated in the Quran, have adopted the right path and, sooner or later, they will reach their destination.

Man cannot afford to ignore these laws. Neither can man set up a parallel system of laws. We have no choice but to discover these laws and plan our activities in accordance with them. Going against these laws will benefit no one, neither men nor women. Here the formula is very simple—either follow the natural path—or perish.

The Importance of Interaction

The Quran holds interaction to be of great importance. Interaction should definitely be engaged in, whatever the situation. This principle is laid down in the chapter *Al-Fath* (Victory). The translation of the relevant verses is as follows:

> Truly, We have granted you a clear victory, so that God may forgive you your past and future sins and complete His favour to you and guide you to a straight path, and so that God might bestow on you His mighty help. (48:1-3)

These Quranic verses have a historical background. The Prophet of Islam started a mission in Arabia, which was completely peaceful. But at that time people did not have the religious freedom that we have today. They were, therefore, greatly angered by his initiatives and ultimately started a war against him.

A war-like situation did not favour the Prophet. He wanted to convey his message to everyone but, with such adverse circumstances, all normal contacts were almost totally severed. This was particularly acute on the occasion of the confrontation between the Prophet and his companions and the non-Muslim forces at Hudaybiyyah. The Prophet and his followers wanted to proceed to Makkah from Hudaybiyyah to perform their religious rites at the Kaaba. But the other party stopped them from doing so. The Prophet, wanting quite naturally to normalize the situation, initiated peace talks between the two parties, which lasted two weeks. These have been recorded in history as the Hudaybiyyah Treaty.

Interaction should definitely be engaged in, whatever the situation.

The Prophet discovered that the other party, with their negative mindset, was in no way ready to halt their militancy. He offered, therefore, to accept all their conditions unilaterally, provided that they agreed to end the hostilities. This offer was accepted, resulting in a ten-year no-war pact between the two parties.

When this peace treaty was finalized, God revealed the verses given above in the Quran. At face value, the Hudaybiyyah Treaty was like a defeat, for the price paid by the Prophet was his unilateral acceptance of all the conditions laid down by the other party. But the Quran, in the above verses, declared it as a 'clear victory'. In what sense was it a clear victory? The answer is quite obvious. The Hudaybiyyah Treaty successfully removed the deadlock and opened the door to peaceful interaction between the two parties.

The result showed that this had been a piece of master-strategy. Where the war-time situation had suspended all kinds of interaction, after the peace treaty the door to interaction was thrown wide open. It is a fact that where there is interaction there is discussion, and where there is discussion, there is ideological exchange, and where there is ideological exchange, there is every opportunity to establish one's ideological supremacy over the other party. And that is exactly what happened.

A few years after the signing of this treaty, almost the whole of Arabia accepted the ideology of the Prophet of Islam. Peaceful combat through ideology proves to be far more effective than the might of the sword.

The Hudaybiyyah experience was not simply a matter of religion. It is relevant to all the affairs of human life. It gives us a master formula to manage all controversial matters, within the family and in society, as well as at the national level. If you are facing violent extremism from opponents, make them ready to establish peace, even if it means accepting their conditions unilaterally. In the long run, due to the ensuing peaceful relationship, you will be a success.

The Creation Plan of God

*E*veryone asks the same questions: Who am I? Why I am here on this planet earth? What is the purpose of man? What is success and what is failure? These questions may be summed up in a single sentence: What is the creation plan of the Creator? Chapter sixty-seven of the Quran, *Al-Mulk* (The Kingdom), gives the answer to this question. The translation of the relevant verse is as follows:

> God created death and life so that He might test you, and find out which of you is best in conduct. He is the Mighty, the Most Forgiving One. (67:2)

According to the Quran, man was created as an eternal being. In the above Quranic verse 'death and life' represent both the pre-death period of life and the post-death period of human life. So, death and life cover the entire eternal life span of human beings.

The fact is that God created man with a well thought-out plan, the essence of which is to give man complete freedom—not simply as a gift, but as a test. The result of this test would enable God to know who misused his freedom and who put his freedom to the best use. This was, and still is, the divine scheme of things for man.

This test is not just for the sake of testing mankind. It is for a high purpose. Before creating man, God created an ideal world, that is, Paradise. Now God wanted ideal men and women who would merit being settled in this Paradise for all eternity. Therefore, the present world is a selection ground for Paradise.

According to this divine scheme, the present human lifetime affords a great opportunity to man. In the pre-death period of life, man has the chance to qualify himself for Paradise, so that in the post-death period of life he may be settled as a deserving candidate in this perfect world.

This divine scheme gives man great hope. The present world may be one of problems, for in this world there are sorrows, pains and unwanted situations. But the divine scheme of life prescribed in the Quran gives us a great solace. It is like a bright light in the darkness. It gives men and women great hope that all those sorrows they experience in the present world are for the temporary period of testing, and that once they qualify in the test, they will be fortunate candidates for eternal Paradise.

This Quranic notion explains human life. It explains not only the existence of man, but also all the misadventures that he faces in this world. It gives great meaning to all the good and the bad in life.

Man is born with unique qualities, he is born with unlimited desires, his mind has enormous capacity but, before realizing his potential and before fulfilling his desires, his life comes to an end.

This divine scheme gives man great hope. The present world may be one of problems, for in this world there are sorrows, pains and unwanted situations. But the divine scheme of life prescribed in the Quran gives us a great solace.

Given his often untimely demise, man seems to be a completely inexplicable phenomenon, but in the light of the above divine scheme, human life becomes completely explainable and understandable. Keeping this in mind, one sees how everything falls into place.

Making the Right Choice

The chapter *Al-Tin* (The Fig) of the Quran is very short, but it has a great lesson, a universal message for all men and woman—an eternal formula for a successful life. The translation of the relevant verses is as follows:

We have indeed created man in the best of moulds,
then We cast him down as the lowest of the low.
(95:4-5)

Anyone who goes through these verses will discover great
meaning in them. Everyone by nature has a unique personality,
but nothing in this world is all good—the human personality has
minus points as well as plus points. One who makes the most of
his plus points is successful, whereas one who becomes a victim
of his minus points is doomed to failure.

The plus and minus points can be summed up under the
headings of reason and emotion. One who obeys reason achieves
success, while one who is lead by his emotions is bound to face
disaster. Reason, implying unbiased thinking, leads to a realistic
approach. It makes you a mature person and guides you to
give well-considered responses and to plan all your actions in a
rational way. A life which is based on reason is invariably marked
by success and salvation.

*The emotional approach is not a very simple one
and can come at a great cost. Dealing with things
emotionally is like mishandling glassware.*

The emotional approach is only another name for an
irrational approach. One who is swayed by his emotions becomes
unrealistic in his dealings. His actions are typified by the well-
known saying: 'Fools rush in where angels fear to tread.' With a
single word-change, the formula goes like this: 'Emotional people
rush in where angels fear to tread.'

The emotional approach is not a very simple one and can
come at a great cost. Dealing with things emotionally is like
mishandling glassware. You can mishandle ironware, but you
cannot behave like that with glassware, because it might fall down
and be smashed. In any human situation, you have similarly to

handle matters with great care, otherwise the result will be like the smashing of delicate glassware. If this happens, it will lead to a breakdown in relationships and you cannot afford such a breakdown.

The human personality, a unique combination of mind and body, is a great boon for every man and woman. If you use your personality to the best advantage, you will become a super achiever. But then there is the other possibility, that is, of putting your personality to the wrong use. Misusing your personality is like mishandling glassware. You are doomed to paying a heavy price for doing so. But, if properly used, it will lead to super achievement. Improper use will lead to dismal failure.

There are numerous creatures in this world, but out of all of them, man is quite unique in having freedom of choice. Freedom of choice is a valuable asset that elevates man to the highest rank. But freedom of choice is a double-edged sword. It may kill your enemy but at the same time it can kill you too. So, while one who is extremely cautious can become a universal hero, one who opts for rash, ill-considered courses of action will be reduced to a total zero.

The Value of Differences

Uniformity is not the culture of our world. This lack of uniformity is observable all over the world. The Quran affirms this fact. It says that the stones of the mountains are different in colour (35:27), in plants there are diverse varieties (20:53), and the same picture is observable in the animal world. Regarding man, the Quran, in the chapter Al-Rum (The Romans) has this to say:

Another of His signs is that He created the heavens and earth, and the diversity of your languages and colours. There truly are signs in this for those who know. (30:22)

It is a fact that our life is full of differences. In fact, every man is Mr. Different and every woman is Ms. Different. Diversity is an integral part of nature and is immutable.

What to do in such a situation? The only option in this case is to adopt the principle of tolerance. Maturity is the ability to accept things that we cannot change. And every man and woman should prove to be a mature person in this regard.

In such a situation, everyone should learn the art of difference management, rather than try to eliminate the differences, for this can lead to nothing but failure.

Difference is not an evil: it has a great positive value. Difference is a challenge. Difference awakens the mind.

Difference management is not a difficult task. In terms of the capacity of the human mind, it is certainly an easy task. Regarding the capacity of the mind, it has rightly been said: "I am large enough to contain all these contradictions."

Difference is not an evil: it has a great positive value. Difference is a challenge. Difference awakens the mind. Difference invites discussion and dialogue. And, dialogue and discussion lead to intellectual development. Difference saves us from being a victim of intellectual stagnation.

There is a saying: "If all think alike, no one thinks very much." This saying aptly explains the value of difference. Uniformity is not part of the scheme of nature. The scheme of nature is based on diversity rather than uniformity.

Tolerance is not a passive attitude. Tolerance is an amalgam of all kinds of noble values, such as exercising patience, giving respect to others, forbearance, deep wisdom, and the willingness to co-exist with others. These qualities are what make up a good person. One who is lacking in the spirit of tolerance is bereft of all kinds of human values.

Distraction from worthwhile objectives is a fatal lapse in any man or woman, but the spirit of tolerance saves one from such deviation. One who is tolerant will certainly be spared unpleasant situations, while one who is intolerant will find himself involved in all manner of things that are not to his liking. Individuals who are intolerant, both men and women, are bound to ruin their lives—partially if not totally.

Tolerance means giving a well-considered response in any given situation. It is the sign of a sound mind. A person of sound mind is one who refrains himself from instant reaction, who tries to examine the situation, who judges the pros and cons of his actions, and only then does he give his response. This is the spirit of tolerance; and tolerance is the sign of a wise person.

A Course in Self-Control

In the chapter *Al-Baqarah* (The Heifer) of the Quran, believers are enjoined to fast during the month of Ramadan, fasting being one of the five pillars of the religion of Islam. The translation of the relevant verse is as follows:

> Believers, fasting has been prescribed for you, just as it was prescribed for those before you, so that you may guard yourselves against evil. (2:183)

What is meant by fasting? In this context, it is to abstain

from eating and drinking for one whole month. The period of fasting begins from sunrise and ends at sunset. Throughout this month, believers can eat and drink during the night, but not in the daytime.

According to Islamic teaching, fasting is not simply about experiencing hunger and thirst. In fact, hunger and thirst are symbolic of purifying one's soul and training oneself to control one's desires. The Prophet of Islam has said to this effect that one, who fails to abstain from using abusive language and persists in his evil habits, will not have his abstinence from eating and drinking accepted by God.

The fact is that everyone has enormous desires, everyone has an ego and there are so many negative thoughts hidden in the human heart. To live the life of a true believer, one is required to control one's desires and to try to live a life of self-restraint.

By giving up eating and drinking in the month of Ramadan, one tries to train oneself for a greater form of fasting, that is, refraining from all kinds of evil habits. Psychological studies show that if someone forms a habit over a period of a whole month, this habit becomes a part of his second nature. In one sense, fasting in the month of Ramadan is based on this human psychology, which is used to bring about moral training.

To live the life of a true believer, one is required to control one's desires and to try to live a life of self-restraint.

Self-disciplined behaviour has the greatest value in the life of a man or a woman. Self-discipline makes one a predictable person and a good member of society. Self-discipline makes one a man of principle, thus enabling one to perform one's duties. Self-discipline develops a mature personality and makes it possible for one's potential to be utilized in significant ways. Self-discipline, in helping one to evolve as a developed personality, is the key to all kinds of success. It saves one from provocation, anger and unnecessary involvement. It is a master formula by which one can manage all the affairs of one's life. Without self-discipline, one is like an animal, whereas with self-discipline one becomes a man in the complete sense of the word. Self-discipline, in setting bounds to one's freedom, helps one to manage one's desires and checks one from going astray.

Self-discipline is an act of the present, but it brings one great benefit in the future. Self-discipline is the best formula for future building. It saves one from saying: "Alas, I missed the bus!"

The Phenomenon of Degeneration

*M*uslims, like other religious communities, went through a phase of degeneration in their later period and matters have not improved in the present day. What to do when this happens? The remedy was outlined in advance in the chapter *Al-Hadid* (Iron) of the Quran. The translation of the relevant verses is as follows:

> Has the time not come for the faithful when their hearts in all humility should engage in the remembrance of God and of the revelation of truth, so that they should not become like those who were given the Book before them, whose hearts with the passage of time became hardened and many of whom were disobedient? Remember that God brings the earth back to life after its death. We have made Our signs clear to you, so that you may fully understand. (57:16-17)

These Quranic verses refer to the period of decline of the *ummah* (Muslim community). This degeneration has come about because the members of the Muslim community have lost their fear of God and have become insensitive to their faith. So, what is the formula for their regeneration, or their reform, so that they may be brought back on to the right path?

The formula is given here in terms of an example from agriculture. With the passage of time, land which had been fertile becomes barren. When the farmer tries to make his land fertile again, he begins his task by preparing the land and not by harvesting. If he starts his job by harvesting, it would be like putting the cart before the horse.

At that time Muslims need to revive their faith, to rediscover the living ideology of Islam and to re-awaken their minds along the lines which were followed by the Prophet and his companions.

The same is true of the declining Muslim community. Here, reformers must start their task from the beginning, and not from the end. For example, if they try in such circumstances to establish their political rule, it will not work. But if they start by reviving the spirit of religion, awakening the soul, and bringing about intellectual development, then it will be a right beginning.

The decline of an *ummah* means decline in terms of spirit, and not in terms of form. Forms or rituals have always been in existence: what disappears is the spirit. So, it is the spirit that needs to be revived, and not merely forms or rituals.

What is degeneration? Degeneration is simply a kind of detachment. When people forget the original message of Islam and cling merely to some lifeless rituals—that is the sign of degeneration.

At that time Muslims need to revive their faith, to rediscover the living ideology of Islam and to re-awaken their minds along the lines which were followed by the Prophet and his companions. It is this act which is called in the Hadith (saying of the Prophet) *tajdeed*, or revival.

The process of *tajdeed* cannot be successful if the reformers want simply to revive the ritualistic form of Islam. The above example of the barren land tells us that the starting point for reform is intellectual awakening and not simply the revival of ritualistic practices.

Moreover, the task of revival needs a creative approach entailing the use of the contemporary idiom; reformers should try to sense their listeners' moods and preach in such a manner that their minds may be addressed. If people's minds are not addressed, then no reform movement will yield any positive results.

The Prophet's Life was an Open Book

According to the Quran, the Prophet of Islam lived an exemplary life. Different aspects of the prophetic character are described in the Quran, one of which is alluded to in the chapter *Yunus* (Jonah). The translation of the relevant verse is as follows:

> Say, 'If God had so wished, I would not have recited it to you, nor would He have brought it to your knowledge. Indeed, I have spent a whole lifetime among you before it came to me. How can you not use your reason?' (10:16)

According to this Quranic verse, the Prophet's life was an open book. His character was known to everyone in minute detail. No chapter of his life's book was hidden from his contemporaries. He was accessible to everyone at all times. He was available to answer people's questions. His life was as transparent as glass. Even his enemies could not say of him that there was any contradiction between his private life and his public life.

This was not simply a personal matter. It had great social value. Leading a blameless life and having sterling qualities makes one predictable and encourages others to accept one as a trustworthy person. It was due to such a character, the Prophet projected such a noble image in Makkah that people gave him the very exceptional title of *al-sadiq al-amin*, that is, the truthful and trustworthy.

According to this Quranic verse, the Prophet's life was an open book. His character was known to everyone in minute detail.

It was this flawless character of the Prophet that prevented anyone in ancient Arabia from saying: "O Prophet, you are telling a lie, we cannot believe that your claim of being a Prophet of God is true." When he proclaimed that God had appointed him as a prophet, no one was able to deny his claim. This miracle of his acceptance was wrought purely by the sublimity of his character. Almost all those who had a close relationship with him, and were well informed about his life, accepted him as a Prophet at the very first instance, either publicly or privately.

Once a Makkan leader met the Prophet and told him that the Makkans had reservations about what he had to say about divine revelations, because they had never witnessed an angel of God coming to him to reveal the word of God. But he added:

"O Muhammad, we do not say that you are telling a lie. So far as your integrity is concerned, we have no doubt about it."

The Prophet is a role model for everyone who believes in his prophethood. Character of this calibre establishes one's identity in the eyes of both God and the people. But such a character is not the sole privilege of a prophet. Every single believer can have such a character and is certainly expected to emulate the character of the Prophet.

The Prophet's veracity was almost a byword in Makkah. The following is a portion of a dialogue between the Christian Emperor Heraclius and Abu Sufyan, an opponent of the Prophet at that time:

Emperor Heraclius: "Did you suspect him of lying before he said what he said?"

Abu Sufyan: "No."

Emperor Heraclius: "And does he break his pledges?"

Abu Sufyan: "No."

Emperor Heraclius: "If he does not lie to man, then how will he lie to God Almighty?"

This dialogue shows the sheer strength of a person's character. Indeed, you are known to your neighbours by your character and not by anything else.

Respect All Cultures, Do Not Discriminate

God Almighty sent more than one hundred thousand prophets or messengers to every group of people. All the messengers of God enjoy the same equal status. There is a verse in the Quran to this effect. In the chapter *Al-Baqarah* (The Heifer), the Quran, referring to these messengers, says:

> The Messenger believes in what has been sent down to him from his Lord, and [so do] believers. They all believe in God and His angels, His scriptures, and His messengers. They say, 'We do not differentiate between any of His messengers. We hear and obey. Grant us Your forgiveness, Lord, to You we shall all return!' (2:285)

This Quranic verse relates directly to the messengers or the prophets of God, but it also has a broader application, according to which everyone is worthy of respect, regardless of his creed or culture.

A healthy society is not necessarily a uni-religious society; a healthy society is one which is based on religious freedom and religious tolerance.

Such belief promotes a culture of equal respect among mankind. Difference in belief is necessarily subject to discussion, but it is not a reason for discrimination. If your belief system is different from that of others, you have every right to engage in discussion and dialogue on the subject, but in the process you have no right to show disrespect to others. This holds true, even if you feel that your personal ideology enshrines the supreme truth. The culture of discrimination is, after all, quite alien to the divine religion.

Islam has two aims regarding society—dissemination of the truth as set forth in the Quran, and maintaining a healthy society that honours the principles of respect and peaceful co-existence. To this end, the Quran lays great emphasis on restraint and discipline—conflict and extremism being completely alien to the Islamic system of thought.

In everyday life, everyone should be disciplined and bow to the principle of tolerance, for others have a right to live according to their convictions, just as I want to live according to my own convictions. This is the best way to build a healthy society. A healthy society is not necessarily a uni-religious society; a healthy society is one which is based on religious freedom and religious tolerance.

Mutual respect is not simply of moral value; it is also a great source of intellectual advancement. When you tolerate the ideology of others, you give others free rein to express their views, thus creating an atmosphere conducive to positive discussion and peaceful dialogue. And, positive discussion and peaceful dialogue invariably lead to intellectual challenges and ideological questioning. Respect for all cultures is, therefore, a factor which is greatly supportive of all kinds of intellectual development.

The most important aspect of having respect for all cultures is that it eliminates all kinds of negative thinking. It helps you to discover the beauty of others' thinking and way of life, which is vital if a healthy society is to be established.

No Conflict Between Prayer and Commerce

According to the Quranic scheme of life, there is no difference between prayer and commerce. The Quran does not believe in drawing a line of demarcation between the two. Both the activities are divine, provided the believer observes the commandments of God. In the chapter *Al-Jumu'ah* (The Day of Congregation), the Quran says:

> Believers! When the call to prayer is made on the day of congregational prayer, hasten to the remembrance of God, and leave all worldly commerce: this is for your own good, if you but knew it. When the prayer is ended, disperse in the land and seek to obtain [something] of God's bounty; and remember God much, so that you may prosper. (62:9-10)

This Quranic verse makes it clear that people are allowed to engage in commerce before the call of prayer; and after the completion of prayer, they are again allowed to go about their business. So these two activities are not at variance with each other.

A believer is one who discovers the Quranic truth as a complete theory of life. This belief is manifested in his worldly life as well as in that part of his life that is defined as being purely religious.

According to the Quran, the essence of religion is living in the remembrance of God. Prescribed prayer is a formal kind of remembrance of God, but in the course of commercial activities, believers are again required to keep remembering God, for—in the religion of Islam—without doing so, life is lacking in any religious virtue. Religion and worldly activities are only different faces of the same coin; the true believer discovers this divine truth. This discovery is so strong that it brings about a great change in the believer's life; it revolutionizes his mind and heart. Such a person becomes an all-time believer, day and night, morning and evening. When he is engaged in formal worship, he is mentally remembering God Almighty and when he is carrying on his trade, or is busy in any other worldly activity, he is again engaged in God's remembrance. In this sense there is no dichotomy in the believer's life, for his personality is holistic in nature. This is the true concept of the Quranic life.

This formula pertains not only to the day of congregation prayer: it gives, in fact, the complete scheme laid down for the believer. According to the Quran, belief is not simply a creed to be observed ritually. It is a complete formula for the whole life of the believer.

A believer is one who discovers the Quranic truth as a complete theory of life. This belief is manifested in his worldly life as well as in that part of his life that is defined as being purely religious. A believer is a believer during his worldly activities as well as during his religious practices.

The Quranic religion is a mind-based religion; this means that the Quran revolutionizes the whole personality of the believer in such a way that his intentions, his thinking, his behaviour, his external conduct are all dyed in the same divine colour. He is a believer when he is in a place of worship and he is also a believer when he is in the market or any other worldly place. The criterion of a true believer is his soul and not his external form.

When You Make a Mistake

One of the Quranic teachings is *tawbah*, which means repentance. When you make a mistake and do *tawbah*, the blessing of God will return to you. In the chapter *Al-Tahrim* (Prohibition), the Quran says:

> O believers, turn to God in sincere repentance, in the hope that your Lord will forgive you your bad

deeds and admit you into gardens watered by running streams. (66:8)

In this verse the Quran declares that after engaging in genuine *tawbah*, one who has erred will be unburdened of the effect of his bad deeds. What is most important about this is that the wrong-doer will be granted forgiveness by God and will consequently be rewarded with Paradise in the hereafter. This divine blessing is not confined to the next world; in the extended sense, it also includes the present world. Family life and social life will also be blessed with the fruits of *tawbah*.

If you make a mistake that arouses anger in another, but then you repent and say: "Please forgive me, I was wrong," this will certainly cause the aggrieved person to have a change of heart. Such an apology will, on the one hand, inculcate positivity in your soul and, on the other, it will promote the culture of love among the people you are living with.

Tawbah is an instrument of self-correction, initiating a process of self re-assessment. This process is vital, as it enhances your intellectual calibre and increases your capacity for analysis.

In family life as well as social life, untoward events are unavoidable. Such happenings sour relations and create a distance between people. The best solution is *tawbah*. Don't wait for others to take the lead. It is for you to come forward and say without hesitation: "I'm sorry, I was wrong." This is the only way of maintaining normalcy among relatives, friends, acquaintances and even strangers.

Problems in social life invariably arise from some kind of wrong behaviour. In reality, men are by nature egoists and women are emotional. The simple solution to having a tranquil social life is not to ruffle the ego of a man and not to neglect a woman's emotions. There is no social ill that cannot be set right by this two-point formula. But it must also be accepted that to err is human, so whenever you err and some man or woman becomes negative towards you, do not hesitate but at once admit your mistake and say: "Sorry, I was wrong." This short sentence will prove to be magical in its effect and the whole situation will instantly be normalized. This is the miracle of *tawbah*.

Tawbah is an instrument of self-correction, initiating a process of self re-assessment. This process is vital, as it enhances your intellectual calibre and increases your capacity for analysis. This, in turn, leads to spiritual development.

People have no difficulty in saying: "O God, forgive me." But when it comes to a human problem, they are reluctant to say: "O brother, please forgive me." This kind of hesitation is against the spirit of faith. A true man of faith will say to another: "Forgive me," just as easily as he says to God: "O Lord, forgive me." *Tawbah* is an inner spirit, a readiness to atone for every kind of mistake.

It is Quality that Matters

In the chapter *Al-Baqarah* (The Heifer), the Quran sets forth an important law of nature, which pertains to the most important factors in life's struggle. The translation of the relevant verse is as follows:

> But those of them who believed that they would meet God replied, 'Many a small group, by God's command, has prevailed against a large group. For God is with those who are patient in adversity.' (2:249)

According to this Quranic verse, in the quantification of virtues, there are two factors in life which are of prime importance—belief and patience. These two factors are more telling than any number of other virtues. So we have to pay more attention to inculcating these two qualities, belief and patience, rather than simply trying to increase the number of other virtues that we possess.

What is a majority or a large group? It is a composite of individuals. If the individual is strong, the group will be strong, and if the individual is weak, then the group will also be weak. The individual is like a brick. And it takes many bricks to put up a building. If each single brick is strong, the building will in consequence be strong, but if even a single brick is weak, the whole building will also prove to be weak and could come tumbling down.

It is a fact that strength lies in individuals and not in the group. A group itself is nothing. It is individuals or members of groups, who determine the strength of the group and not the group itself.

The above Quranic verse makes special mention of two qualities in an individual—belief and patience. The former underpins the ideological strength of an individual, while the latter reinforces his strength in practical matters. These two features are indispensable.

It is a fact that strength lies in individuals and not in the group. It is individuals or members of groups, who determine the strength of the group and not the group itself.

Ideology is the mainspring of a man's intellectual strength. Whatever ideology he subscribes to gives him conviction and courage and, moreover, vision; one who possesses these qualities is undoubtedly a complete person. He is able to think, he is able to take decisions, he is able to go into the deeper aspects of situations and make objective assessments. He is able to say in the face of adversity: "I will surmount it."

Patience is a very important quality. Life is full of problems and untoward events, so you have to avoid being a victim of provocation and, going beyond immediate circumstances, refrain from any reactionary approach. Only a patient person is in a position to practice the necessary self-restraint. Only a patient person can go beyond his immediate circumstances and properly plan his life by taking into consideration every relevant factor on a long-term basis.

Only a patient person is able to do future-oriented planning, and it is future-oriented planning that leads to great success. In life's struggle, there are frequent occasions when immediate decision-making becomes essential. This being so, every member of the group must be a programme maker, and not just a programme receiver. Super achievement is destined only for groups whose members have this kind of superior quality. A large group consisting of weak individuals is vulnerable like a balloon, while a small group with strong members is rock-like in its strength.

Just Speech and Correct Conduct

The chapter *Al-Ma'idah* (The Table) of the Quran gives guidance on correct conduct in matters of justice. The translation of the relevant verse is as follows:

> Believers, be steadfast in the cause of God and bear witness with justice. Do not let your enmity for others turn you away from justice. Deal justly; that is nearer to being God-fearing. Fear God. God is aware of all that you do. (5:8)

It is good to observe moral standards in whatever you have to say in normal situations. But that is not enough. The real test comes when the situation is adverse in the sense of being abnormal or provocative. It is how you conduct yourself in such a situation that proves whether you are one who speaks with justice or not.

In a normal situation anyone can adhere to moral values, but the real test of a worthy person is his having the capacity to speak with justice even in very difficult situations.

In provocative situations, people generally react unjustly. They take the provocative aspect of situations as an excuse for their unjust speech or their unjust behaviour, but this kind of excuse does not measure up to the Quranic standard of morality. The Quranic principle in this regard can be formulated in these words: "If you have a good excuse, don't use it."

In a normal situation anyone can adhere to moral values, but the real test of a worthy person is his having the capacity to speak with justice even in very difficult situations.

Society can be torn apart by differences and undesirable situations. Even the best of things may turn out to be bad for others and this is what arouses anger and provocative behaviour. This disrupts normalcy, and if people get into the habit of making excuses for their own bad behaviour, every society will become a morass of hatred and intolerance.

If the members of society figure as Mr. Excuse or Ms. Excuse, society will be a permanent jungle. So, the above criterion of justice is not simply a bastion of morality but it is also the sole factor that can maintain a reasonable degree of normalcy in human society.

The adoption of this principle is a sign not of passivity but of maturity. When a member of society speaks out for justice, even when this could favour his enemy, he is not showing a passive attitude but is demonstrating his maturity. It means that he is a wise person who can control his negative emotions.

Avoiding enmity is not simply a piece of strategy designed to outwit your enemy. It is a positive mode of conduct which enhances your spirituality and is a sign of high moral standards. It helps in developing your personality, gives you fresh experiences, and increases your creativity. After conducting yourself in this way, you will emerge as a healthy mind.

To speak with justice is the only option in this world. Any other option is disastrous. It is not a matter of choice; it is a matter of compulsion. Our world is controlled by the law of nature, and the law of nature does not allow any other kind of behaviour: you cannot afford to go against the law of nature. When you speak with justice in a negative situation, you only have to control your emotions, but when you go against the law of nature, you are on the path to destroying your life.

Discrimination is Alien to the Quran

Discrimination of any kind is quite alien to the scheme of things in the Quran. In the chapter *Al-Hujurat* (The Apartments), the Quran declares that all men and women are equal before God. The translation of the relevant verse is as follows:

Mankind! We have created you from a male and female, and made you into peoples and tribes, so that you might come to know each other. The noblest of you in God's sight is the one who fears God most. God is all-knowing and all-aware. (49:13)

There are obvious differences between people in terms of colour, race, economic status, etc., but according to the Quran, the difference is simply a difference: it cannot be used as a basis for discrimination.

God Almighty created man with different attributes, difference being a part of creation. Differences exist for practical rather than theoretical reasons. Their main purpose is to enable people to recognize and distinguish one from another.

In other words, differences among people are a healthy sign. It is due to these differences that we recognize each other and carry out our dealings on this basis. If there were complete uniformity—with all human beings cast in exactly the same mould—then it would be very difficult to live in society in a normal manner.

Differences among people are a healthy sign. It is due to these differences that we recognize each other and carry out our dealings on this basis.

It is a fact that difference is a part of nature. But if we were to take difference in the sense of discrimination, that would be an unhealthy sign and would disturb the normalcy of society. So we have to learn the art of difference management, rather than look upon differences in any negative sense.

Then there are other benefits of difference, due to which people take up a variety of jobs, entering different fields of activity. Difference provides the basis for the division of labour, a principle which is very important for the comprehensive development of any society.

According to the divine scheme, honour is based on merit and not on any kind of external features. The Prophet of Islam once said that, before God, red and white, black and brown, were all equal. He said: "Behold, God has removed from you the arrogance of pagan ignorance (*jahiliyyah*) with its boast of ancestral glories. Man is but a God-conscious believer or an unfortunate sinner. All people are children of Adam, and Adam was created out of dust."

There may be differences in colour or physical features, but man is what he is in his inner being and, in this sense, everyone has the same potential. Everyone is born with the same inner qualities, so one who discovers himself and tries to turn his potential into a reality is the one who will be successful.

You are not what others think you are: you are what you prove yourself to be. Everyone has the capacity to become a self-made man. Everyone has the capacity to dispel others' misunderstandings about him, and the Creator expects you to make use of this capacity. God has not shown any discrimination between different people. It is men and women themselves who give others the chance to discriminate against them.

Political Status Quoism

How is political power defined in the Quran? It is clearly set forth in the chapter *Al-'Imran* (The Family of Imran). The translation of the relevant verse is as follows:

> Say, 'Lord, sovereign of all sovereignty. You bestow sovereignty on whom You will and take it away from whom You please; You exalt whoever You will and abase whoever You will. All that is good lies in Your hands. You have the power to will anything. (3:26)

According to this Quranic statement, political power is a gift of God. It cannot be achieved through fighting or conquest. If anyone tries to capture political power by dethroning the existing ruler, it is against the law of nature, and any endeavour of this kind is doomed to failure. Sooner or later, it will prove to be disastrous.

This formula given in the Quran can be summarized in two words: political status quoism, that is, acceptance of the political situation and waiting for your turn to come. If someone achieves political power by God's decision, it will prove to be good for him, but if he tries to snatch power from others, it will prove to be counterproductive.

This Quranic formula means that in political matters, you must first consider the result of your endeavours. Your struggle must be result-oriented and not simply ambition-oriented.

The principle of status quoism is not the result of passivity or cowardice: it is the result of the greatest wisdom. When you accept the political status quo, you instantly find time for your work. But if you try to change the political status quo through fighting and violence, you will lose all available opportunities.

This Quranic formula means that in political matters, you must first consider the result of your endeavours. Your struggle must be result-oriented and not simply ambition-oriented. Do not look to your own political desires, but anticipate the actual result by objectively analyzing matters. Then, certainly you will find that the pro-status quo formula is far better than the pro-change formula. When you adopt political status quoism, it is an apparent attempt to adjust to the existing political setup, whereas you are in fact trying to seek adjustment with the laws of nature. You are pursuing the policy of buying time.

According to the law of nature, political rule is not the monopoly of one person or one group; it is bound to change from one group to some other group, so adopting a pro-change policy is wasting your time and energy in terms of the result, while accepting the political status quo is simply waiting for your turn which is bound to come to you, sooner or later.

Politics is not the only important field of human activity. There are many other vital spheres of work, like education, business, industry, social reform, academic learning, scientific research, etc. The formula of political status quoism means taking no action against the prevailing political system and availing of the opportunities that are present in so many other fields. In this sense, political status quoism is the formula that is based on the greatest wisdom.

If you adopt the method of political confrontation, you have to fight the opposing party and fighting invariably yields negative results. However, when you adopt the formula of political status quoism there is no rival group, you do not need to fight against anyone, and you have enough time to try to achieve what is achievable for you.

Jihad in Quran: A Peaceful Ideology

Those who are introduced to the Quran only through the media generally have the impression that the Quran is a book of jihad, and jihad to them is an attempt to achieve one's goal by means of violence.

But this idea is based on a misunderstanding. Anyone who

reads the Quran will easily appreciate that its message has nothing to do with violence.

The Quran gives us an introduction to the divine ideology of peaceful struggle. The method of such a struggle, according to the Quran, is "to speak to them a word to reach their very soul." (4:63)

The Quran is, from beginning to end, a book that promulgates peace and in no way countenances violence. It is true that jihad is one of the teachings of the Quran. But jihad, taken in its correct sense, is the name of peaceful struggle rather than of any kind of violent action. The Quranic concept of jihad is expressed in the following verse: "Do greater jihad (i.e. strive more strenuously) with the help of this (i.e. the Quran)." (25:52).

The Quran gives us an introduction to the divine ideology of peaceful struggle. The method of such a struggle, according to the Quran, is "to speak to them a word to reach their very soul." (4:63)

So, the desired approach, according to the Quran, is one that moves man's heart and mind. This is the mission of the Quran. And this mission can be performed only by means of rational argument. This target can never be achieved by means of violence or armed action.

It is true that there are certain verses in the Quran that give permission to wage war. But these verses are only relevant when a state of war already prevails. Physical combat is meant only for defence at the time of an attack. Indeed, no war is lawful in Islam except for defence. Moreover, such defensive warfare can be engaged in only by an established state.

No individual or organization may on its own wage armed jihad.

The Consequences of Wrong Deeds

The consequences of wrong deeds are invariably evil; no one can disown the bad outcome of his own misdeeds. This is a law of nature, the application of which is explained in the chapter *Al-Talaq* (Divorce) of the Quran:

> How many a town rebelled against the commands of its Lord and His messengers and We called them sternly to account and punished them severely, so they tasted the evil consequences of their conduct and the result of their conduct was ruin. (65:8-9)

There is a well-known formula in the world of physics: every action has an equal and opposite reaction. This formula applies to human life also. If you take a wrong step, you cannot escape its bad results. It is a law of nature from which no man or woman is exempt.

It happens generally that when a wrong-doer has to face the consequences of his wrong-doing, he tries to find a scapegoat. But this kind of scapegoat can be found only in the dictionary and not in real life. When you take a wrong step and after some time the results are undesirable, do not delay in accepting that it is your own fault. You should say quite frankly that you were wrong. If you try to blame others, you will very soon discover that there is no taker for this kind of blame.

If you accept your mistake in such a situation, it will actually benefit you. It will enable you to make a reassessment of the whole matter, and that will in turn enable you to re-plan your strategy. And finally it will enable you—when you have missed the first train—to board the next one.

Man has certain limitations. You may work out a plan with good intentions but, due to miscalculation, you fail to achieve your target. This kind of failure can be forgiven; your excuse on this occasion will be quite acceptable. You can say that your assessment had not been realistic, and that that was why you failed to achieve your target.

But this is not the end of the matter. If this happens, you have to say that you were wrong. Accepting the mistake is the best way out of the difficulty, but if you try to find some scapegoat and try to put all the blame on that supposed scapegoat, it will not work.

If you accept your mistake in such a situation, it will actually benefit you. It will enable you to make a reassessment of the whole matter, and that will in turn enable you to re-plan your strategy.

This kind of explanation is bound to boomerang. If you are facing such a situation, do not try to blame others. Doing so is simply a waste of time, because there is no taker for it. So, as soon as you discover that you have made a mistake, accept it in terms of its consequences; and do so immediately. You have to understand that you may have lost the first chance but that now there is time to avail of a second chance. But success in availing of this second chance depends solely upon your acceptance of your own mistake and not putting the blame on other people.

Let there be no Vain or Sinful Talk

In the chapter *Al-Waqi'ah* (The Inevitable Event) the Quran tells us about Paradise. How people will live in Paradise is portrayed as follows:

> They will not hear therein any vain or sinful talk, only words of peace and tranquillity. (56:25-26)

Paradise of the Hereafter is an ideal society. The present world is like a recruiting ground, in which people are being put to the test. Those who qualify in this test will gain entry to Paradise. The present world is a selecting ground and Paradise is a place where those selected will be settled.

One quality required of the people of Paradise is the ability to refrain from creating a nuisance for others, i.e. the ability to live in society in complete peace and tranquillity. Those who prove that they have the capacity to live according to this norm will be included in the list of those who will be settled in Paradise.

According to the Quran, there are two criteria for anyone to be included in the society of Paradise; the first is that they should live in complete peace, thus ensuring peace and tranquillity for other members of society. Then the second condition is that they should refrain from creating a nuisance for others. In other words, they must prove to be no-problem members of society.

Although the above-mentioned verse is about the society of Paradise, it tells us what kind of social values are acceptable in the present world as well. When we keep in mind that the present world is a selecting ground, then it becomes very clear that in both the places the same ethical norms are required—in the present world as well as in the world hereafter.

So every man and woman must be very cautious in this regard. You must understand that when you create a nuisance for others, it is not simply a problem for those others but is also a great problem for you, because such behaviour will certainly prevent you from being included in the list of those who will enter Paradise. No one can afford to indulge in this kind of behaviour.

How should we define 'nuisance'? Any part of your behaviour that is found undesirable by your fellow beings is a nuisance. You cannot say that you did not act in this manner for the sake of creating a nuisance for others; it is not your opinion that determines what is a nuisance and what is not; it is your fellow beings who have the sole right to determine what is a nuisance and what is not.

One quality required of the people of Paradise is the ability to refrain from creating a nuisance for others, i.e. the ability to live in society in complete peace and tranquillity.

In this situation, you have no excuse; you have no right to say that your intentions were good. In this case, good intentions and bad intentions are not relevant; the only thing that matters is the reaction of your fellow beings. If your behaviour is acceptable to your fellow beings, then it is not a nuisance and if your behaviour is not acceptable to your fellow beings, then it is certainly a nuisance. 'Nuisance' is obviously not a sin. But it is as bad as a sin, because when you hurt the sentiments of your fellow beings, your actions in terms of their results are certainly a sin.

The Importance of Playing a Secondary Role

*I*n the chapter *Al-Zukhruf* (Ornaments of Gold), the Quran describes a law of nature, which is very important for the purpose of nation building. The translation of the relevant verse is as follows:

> Is it they who apportion the blessing of your Lord? It is We who distribute among them their livelihood in the life of this world, and raise some of them above others in rank, so that they may take one another into service; and the blessing of your Lord is better than [the wealth] which they amass. (43:32)

These differences between people are not simply a matter of disparity or discrimination: there is great wisdom behind these differences. They give us a form of direction on how to manage our social system. In simple language, this means that one person must take the primary role and all other members of society must accept a secondary role. This is the only method of organization by means of which a society can achieve its highest targets.

It is a fact that a great achievement requires the joint efforts of a great number of people; a single individual on his own cannot achieve the highest of social goals. So, what is the formula for a successful joint effort of this kind? It is: give one able person the role of leadership, while all other persons take a back seat and play a secondary role.

It is a fact that, without joint efforts, no high goal can be achieved, but joint efforts always need someone at the helm of affairs. Without a boss you cannot run a company, without a prime minister you cannot run a government, without the head of the family you cannot run a home, without a coordinator, or a supervisor, you cannot run a joint effort. Adherence to the principle of leadership is an integral part of any successful joint effort.

This being so, the law of nature set forth in the above Quranic verse is a great blessing for us. God Almighty created people with differences or disparities. It is this difference or disparity that gives us the opportunity to bow to the principle of leadership in our social activities. This principle could not work if all the members of society were completely equal. Equals need a superior person to manage their affairs. This requires them to accept the principle of leadership.

Every train requires an engine for its smooth running. Without an engine, the train would not be able to budge an inch. The same is true of society. Society is like a train which we need to mobilize, but this mobilization cannot be achieved without an engine to lead the way. The same formula that requires physical movement is applicable to social movement; the social train cannot travel towards its goal without an engine.

Adherence to the principle of leadership is an integral part of any successful joint effort.

A secondary role is not an inferior role; it is a role that has a value higher than that of the person primarily in command. The commander will be given only one credit but those who accept the secondary role will be rewarded with double credit because, apart from their normal role, they have proved to have a great ability—ego management. Without learning the art of ego management, no one can successfully play the secondary role.

Needed, a Mixture of Opposites

A true believer has one very special quality: he is able to develop a personality that is a blend of opposites. This quality in a believer is outlined in the Quran in the chapter Al-Fath (Victory). The relevant verse is as follows:

> Muhammad is the Messenger of God. Those who are with him are firm and unyielding towards those who deny the truth, but compassionate towards one another. (48:29)

A believer is compelled to live among different kinds of people. Some are good people, by associating with whom one can receive great benefits in terms of spirituality and positivity; but at the same time there are others who are bad, and continuing to associate with them will be harmful to one's morality and spirituality.

The existence of these opposite kinds of characters, both bad and good, which can be found in every society—perhaps without exception—may prove to be a harmful phenomenon. This is a test for a true believer. He must pass in this test. He must be mature enough not to yield to those who obviously have a bad character and at the same time he must be so well-inclined towards those having a good character as to learn from them and receive from them good advice for the betterment of his life.

Social life in this world is like living in a bush where there are beautiful flowers side by side with harmful thorns. You have to be cautious enough to be able to pluck the flowers without becoming entangled with the thorns. This is a bit like tight-rope walking, which requires great skill if one is not to overbalance. Without this skill, no one can achieve his higher goals.

People of evil character are not entirely worthless people. They can also have a positive role, provided you deal with them with a positive mind. If you can inculcate this positive quality in your personality, then bad people can prove to be good teachers for you from different points of view.

Having a mixture of opposites in one's personality is not beyond one's capacity. It is neither unnatural nor impossible. It is quite natural and completely achievable for a sincere person. Describing this human capacity one Western scholar has rightly said: "I am large enough to contain all these contradictions."

People of evil character are not entirely worthless people. They can also have a positive role, provided you deal with them with a positive mind.

No animal has this quality; it is a unique characteristic bestowed upon man by his Creator. All that is needed is to unfold this quality hidden in every human personality. Being a mixture of opposites is a feature of personality development.

It is not a problem: it is rather an opportunity. A mixture of opposites means having diverse qualities, the most important of which is the wisdom of difference management. It is, moreover a sign of principled behaviour. It is a proof of a person's maturity. The mature person adopts the formula of ignoring the problems and availing of the opportunities. He has the ability to act in a selective manner. He possesses the virtue of high morality. It means that his behaviour is a friendly towards all mankind. He is able to deal with both friend and foe alike.

Political Power: A Responsibility

Solomon, an Israelite prophet as well as a king, was the ruler of Palestine and Syria. While engaged in trying to win over the Queen of Sheba in both the political and religious sense, he asked for the throne of the Queen of Sheba to be brought to him. The queen and her throne were hundreds of miles away at that time, but because he had been endowed with special powers, he expected his order to have immediate effect. The Quran refers to how Solomon responded to his order being instantly complied with in the chapter *Al-Naml* (The Ants) of the Quran. The relevant verse is as follows:

> But one of them who had some knowledge of the Book said, 'I will bring it to you in the twinkling of an eye.' When Solomon saw it placed before him, he exclaimed, 'This is by the grace of my Lord, to test whether I am grateful or ungrateful. Whosoever is grateful, it is for the good of his own self; and whosoever is ungrateful, then surely my Lord is self-sufficient and generous.' (27:40)

This verse illustrates the Quranic concept of political power, i.e. it is not a kind of a worldly blessing; it is a test set by God. Just as everything that one possesses in this world is a test paper, so also is political power a test paper. God Almighty is constantly watching the behaviour of the ruler to ascertain whether he is just or unjust in performing his duties. A king is accountable before God just as the common man is.

According to this Quranic concept, political power is a responsibility rather than any kind of blessing. The possession of political power does not mean that the ruler is a superior person, or that the ruler is the master of his subjects, or that the ruler is great and others are not great. The ruler will be presented—just like all other human beings—before God on the Day of Judgement.

This concept of political rule makes the ruler extremely serious in his official dealings. He must consider himself to be the servant of God and, as such, has no option but to follow the divine principles. The ruler is inherently bound to be modest and a well-wisher of all of his subjects. He has to accept the fact that he is not supreme. Only God Almighty is supreme and it is for the ruler to obey His orders. This means that the ruler is compelled to adopt a culture of simplicity rather than a royal culture in his way of life. He has no time for royal entertainments. He is not allowed to impose his whims as the law of the land. He has only one option and that is to obey God's commandments. Otherwise he should step down from his throne.

The possession of political power does not mean that the ruler is a superior person, or that the ruler is the master of his subjects, or that the ruler is great and others are not great.

For the exemplary ruler, rule is not a source of pride, rule is not a source of superiority, rule is not a mandate to become the master of the people. For him, rule is simply a service to his people and nothing beyond that.

According to this concept, a ruler is the head of an administration. He is a manager of his nation and not the nation's overlord. He has no right to exploit the people and he cannot consider his territory to be his property, but rather, it has been bestowed to him by God for the service of his people.

Conscience Serves as a Corrective to Ego

⁓§§§~

*A*ccording to the Quran, all human beings, both men and women, are born with two opposite moral constituents. The first is mentioned in the chapter Yusuf (Joseph) as al-nafs al-ammara (12:53) and the second is mentioned in the chapter Al-Qiyamah (The Day of Resurrection) as *al-nafs al-lawwama* (75:2).

What are *al-nafs al-ammara* and *al-nafs al-lawwama?* In psychological terms, they are the ego and the conscience—with which everyone is born. Almost all human behaviour is affected by these two features. Negative behaviour is the result of *al-nafs al-ammara* and positive behaviour is the result of *al-nafs al-lawwama.*

The ego, if left uncontrolled, becomes the source of all evil, for it is a highly inflammable part of man. In a normal situation, it remains in a dormant state, but when one's ego is negatively touched, it becomes super ego and the result is breakdown. The best way to avoid an ego problem is not to provoke it. In the absence of provocation, the ego creates no problem. But provoke the ego and it is like setting a lighted match to a powder keg.

By contrast, the conscience is the source of all kinds of good. The conscience checks you from indulging in any evil practices, and if you do indulge in any kind of misdemeanour, the conscience becomes alive and compels you to repent and amend your behaviour. The conscience in this way serves as a corrective to every human personality.

This means that whenever there is any controversy, the outcome is in your own hands. If you provoke the ego of the opposite party, you are bound to taste the bitter results of your action. Your negative action will be followed by a negative reaction, and you shall have to pay the price for your own uncalled for initiatives. The best way to confront controversial situations is to be cautious and to try to activate the conscience of the opposite party. This policy will definitely work. The verdict of your rival's conscience will certainly go in your favour. This is a simple formula for a better life.

The conscience checks you from indulging in any evil practices, and if you do indulge in any kind of misdemeanour, the conscience becomes alive and compels you to repent and amend your behaviour.

No one is a born enemy. Enmity is a relative phenomenon of a personality. It is your own negative action that turns a person into your enemy. If you avoid negative action, the apparent enmity will disappear. Enmity is the product of your own wrong behaviour, and through good behaviour you can make people your dear friends.

The ego and the conscience are both good and healthy parts of the human personality. The ego, in the positive sense, gives you determination; it helps you to build a strong personality and, being one of your greatest strengths, it gives you the courage to face challenges. Learn the art of ego management, and the ego will prove to be a blessing for you.

The conscience is also very important for the development of your personality. The conscience instills in you the spirit of mercy and enables you to differentiate between what is right and what is wrong. Above all, the conscience serves as the moral keeper of your personality.

The Opening Chapter of the Quran

*T*here are 114 chapters in the Quran, some long and some short. The opening chapter, *Al-Fatihah* (The Opening), which serves as a preface to the Quran, comprises of only six short verses. The translation of this chapter is as follows:

> All praise is due to God, the Lord of the Universe; the Beneficent, the Merciful; Lord of the Day of Judgement. You alone we worship, and to You alone we turn for help. Guide us to the straight path: the path of those You have blessed; not of those who have incurred Your wrath, nor of those who have gone astray. (1:1-6)

The first verse of this chapter is: "All praise is due to God, the Lord of the Universe." This is the gist of the Quran. The basic message of the Quran is that man must be grateful to God, man must acknowledge God Almighty. Man must adopt a life that is God-oriented. Alhamdulillah covers all these spiritual values.

God Almighty has created man as the superior form of life. He has provided him with all those favourable things that form the life-support system. He created the earth, which is the only planet favourable to human life. He gave man a mind with enormous potential. It is the miracle of the mind that man was able to create a civilization. All the sciences are but a product of the workings of the mind.

In such a situation, it is but natural that man must acknowledge the Creator by saying, Alhamdulillah. Without this acknowledgement, man has no right to live on this planet earth. It is this acknowledgement that gives one legitimacy to live on

139

the planet earth and enjoy all the bounties created by God in this world.

Then the second verse calls God "the Beneficent, the Merciful." These are also words of acknowledgement. When man discovers the fact that the whole world is so favourable to him that it seems that it was created solely for him, he is compelled to believe that the Creator is not simply a creator: he is a benevolent creator in the complete sense of the word. This discovery only increases the spirit of Alhamdulillah. This discovery imbues him with the spirit of love for God. Not only does he become a believer, but his supreme concern becomes God.

It is the miracle of the mind that man was able to create a civilization. All the sciences are but a product of the workings of the mind.

The third verse of this chapter refers to God as: "Lord of the Day of Judgement." This expression is a natural part of man's belief about God. When God created man, and provided him with so many good things, it was but natural that man should become accountable to his Creator. Those who misuse their freedom will be punished by God and those who use their freedom properly will be rewarded. Every blessing entails responsibility and man is certainly no exception to this rule.

The fourth verse of this chapter reads: "You alone we worship, and to You alone we turn for help." This is the real response by man to his Creator. Man must worship God. When man tries to acknowledge his Lord he automatically bows before Him, that is, he surrenders. And his realization of God compels him to seek God's assistance, because He is a giver and man is a taker in this world. This is the essence of the equation between man and God.

The fifth verse of this chapter reads: "Guide us to the straight path." This is also an automatic response from man to his God.

Man's grasp of reality tells him that the greatest blessing that he may ask from God is right guidance. Right guidance is a must for man. And it is God alone who can set man's foot on the right path. Overwhelmed with his feelings of obligation to his Maker, he says: "O God, show me the right path."

The sixth verse of this chapter reads: "The path of those You have blessed; not of those who have incurred Your wrath, nor of those who have gone astray." This verse is an elaboration of the above verses of the chapter.

Avoid Unnecessary Conflict

The Prophet of Islam started his mission in Makkah in 610 AD. At that time he used to pray by adopting the Kaaba as the *qiblah* (prayer direction). Then in 622 he migrated to Madinah where some Jewish tribes had settled. The Prophet then adopted the Jewish *qiblah* for his prayers over a period of fifteen or sixteen months. Then he again turned his face towards the Kaaba as the *qiblah* for his prayers. This event is referred to in the Quran in the chapter *Al-Baqarah* (The Heifer):

> But even if you should produce every kind of sign for those who have been given the Book, they would never accept your prayer direction, nor would you accept their prayer direction: nor would any of them accept one another's direction. If, after all the knowledge you have been given, you yield to their desires, then, you shall surely become a transgressor. (2:145)

This prophetic example embodies an important principle: avoid unnecessary controversy. At that time, the Jews were a dominant community in Madinah (then known as Yathrib). For centuries they had been using the Dome of the Rock (Jerusalem) as their *qiblah* for prayer. It was sacred not only for the Jewish community but also, because of the Jewish influence, for the non-Jewish community.

In such a situation, adopting the Kaaba as the *qiblah* was rather exceptional. In the early months, the Prophet had wanted to avoid unnecessary controversy, so he adopted the Jewish *qiblah* for his prayers five times a day. From this prophetic event we can derive a general principle, not only with regard to prayers, but in other spheres of life also.

A man with a mission always perseveres and avoids hindrances.

This principle is very important; it saves you from unnecessary conflict. It gives you the opportunity to continue your mission in society without a break. It saves you from wasting your energy and time in futile quarrels. It shows great practical wisdom. And without practical wisdom, you cannot achieve any worthy goal in this world.

A man with a mission cannot afford to engage in unnecessary conflict. As a man of dedication, he is determined about achieving his target. He always starts his activities in properly selected fields and never behaves like a grasshopper, jumping from one thing to another. A man with a mission always perseveres and avoids hindrances.

The above example set by the Prophet is an extreme example of this kind. People are not generally ready to be flexible about matters such as prayer, but the Prophet adopted this formula when dealing with this very sensitive issue of prayer.

This formula is applicable to all the affairs of human life—wife and husband relationship, family affairs, social matters, national and international issues—everywhere there are scenarios of such kind and everywhere this formula is applicable. This formula is a universal formula; in this sense you can say that it is a divine formula. It is applicable to both religious and secular affairs.

Understand Things in Correct Perspective

The chapter *Al-Zumar* (Crowds) of the Quran gives a criterion by which we can recognize those who are endowed with understanding. The translation of the relevant verse is as follows:

> Who listen to what is said and follow what is best in it. These are the ones God has guided; these are the people endowed with understanding. (39:18)

A statement, whether religious or secular, has different aspects to it. You can see it from different angles. No statement about the human condition is ever as simple as 'two plus two equals to four'. So, every statement can be interpreted in different ways. Although each statement has only one real meaning, everyone has the freedom to put a right or a wrong interpretation upon it.

Whether the statement will be taken in its true sense or otherwise is determined not by the wording of the statement itself but by the mind of the listener. If the listener is objective, he knows, taking the statement point by point, how to sort out what is valid and what is invalid. He has the ability to assess and analyze things. Moreover, if he is an honest person, he will take the statement in the right way, without allowing misunderstandings to arise.

The sign of a man of reason is that he has the ability to take the statement in its right perspective. He is free of biased thinking and can take things as they are without going astray.

Anyone who has any claim to being a man of logic and reason must develop this kind of understanding. He must train his mind in such a way that he can understand things in their correct perspective. This is a very great asset for both men and women.

If you want to be a right thinker, you have to train yourself and develop this quality. The first condition of right thinking is that you should be objective and be free of all kinds of bias and prejudices. You must have the ability to analyze things on a logical basis. You must know the difference between what is relevant and what is irrelevant.

The sign of a man of reason is that he has the ability to take the statement in its right perspective. He is free of biased thinking and can take things as they are without going astray.

Moreover, if you are to take things from the correct angle, you must be an intellectually honest person and also possess the quality of modesty. When one fails to understand things in a proper manner, it is not simply a failure of understanding, it is more than that, it is a missed opportunity.

If you take things in the right way, you develop your intellect and your personality. Do not miss the opportunity to do so.

Make yourself a complex-free person and then you will be able to understand things without any difficulty. Make yourself free from arrogance, bias and hatred, and then, according to the above definition, you will become a person who can be described as a man of understanding. It is evident that people of understanding are not born: they are trained. Train yourself and you will become a man of understanding.

Two Sources of Knowledge

*M*an always tries to reason things out. The chapter *Al-Ahqaf* (The Sand Dunes) of the Quran, tells us that there are two genuine sources of authentic knowledge which will enlighten us in this regard. The translation of this verse is as follows:

> Say, 'Have you thought about those you call upon apart from God? Show me what they have created on the earth. Or do they have a share in the heavens? Bring me a Book revealed before this or some other vestige of knowledge, if you are telling the truth. (46:4)

According to this Quranic verse, there are two sources of authentic knowledge—revealed knowledge and scientific knowledge. Revealed knowledge is authentic, because it comes directly from God Almighty. And scientific knowledge is authentic because it is based on the laws of nature. Other than these two sources, there is no third source that may be credited as being reliable.

In this sense, the Quran and nature are like each other's counterparts. What is revealed in the Quran is hidden in nature, and what is in nature is revealed in the Quran in a language understandable to man.

The Quran can be understood by acquiring a good command of the Arabic language or by having recourse to its correct translation. By applying the scientific method, what is hidden in nature can be understood by unfolding it.

In other words, there are two sources of knowledge—religious knowledge and secular knowledge. Religious knowledge is based on divine revelation and secular knowledge is based on scientific discovery. One, who wants to be a right thinker, must acquire these two kinds of knowledge. All other knowledge besides these two kinds is speculative and not authentic.

The above-mentioned two kinds of knowledge are not totally different. They are, in fact, complementary to each other. Revealed knowledge justifies scientific knowledge and scientific knowledge confirms revealed knowledge. And both are necessary for intellectual development.

We should peruse this book with complete sincerity, so that we may learn of the basic principles of creation, the real direction of human activities and the right goal for mankind.

It can be said that revealed knowledge is a body of basic facts, while scientific knowledge goes into greater detail about them. It is impossible to find any point on which they contradict each other, provided revealed knowledge is preserved in its original form and scientific knowledge is established by following the method of strictly scientific inquiry.

The above Quranic verse points to the right course of study. First, we have to read the revealed book. We should peruse this book with complete sincerity, so that we may learn of the basic principles of creation, the real direction of human activities and the right goal for mankind.

Then we have to use scientific knowledge as a supportive factor. In fact, science is a Dictionary of Creation and this dictionary is very helpful in understanding the Book sent by the Creator, God Almighty. So, both are equally important for having the right knowledge.

If you study matters objectively and also in the questing spirit, you will find that there is no difference between the two sources of knowledge. Both are equally effectual in the discovery of the truth.

Intellectual Partners

According to Islamic teachings, both men and women are equal in status. In fact, men and women are two equal halves of a single unit. Both are intellectual as well as spiritual partners to each other. In the chapter *Al-'Imran* (The Family of Imran), the Quran emphasizes this principle. The relevant Quranic verse is as follows:

> Their Lord accepted their prayer, saying, 'I will deny no man or woman among you the reward of their labours. You are members one of another.' (3:195)

'Members one of another' does not mean that both are one and the same in every respect. It does not mean that both are each other's counterparts. It means rather that both are made in such a way that they can play a complementary role to each other. So, both are complementary partners to each other rather than each other's counterparts.

There is a saying: "If all think alike, no one thinks very much." So, uniformity between men and women could never have been good for mankind. The creation of man or woman is based then not on uniformity but on difference. Due to this, each is capable of becoming a useful partner for the other.

According to the divine scheme, man and woman were made on the principle of mutual support. Both are intellectual partners to each other; both can discuss and exchange with their partners ideas and experiences. According to the divine scheme, marriage is a communion of two such partners.

Man and woman are like two wheels. A cart runs on two wheels. Such is the case of human life: human life also needs two wheels to run smoothly and man and woman after marriage provide those two wheels. The wheels may be on different sides of the cart but they both play important roles and both are completely equal. There is no inequality between the two.

Life, to be worth living, requires a number of vital inputs, such as education, an understanding of life's moral principles and a willingness to uphold them. Those men and women who are educated and who are trained in home discipline are better qualified to play their respective roles. Education equips both to serve as worthy partners.

The home is a single unit of society and society is a combination of different homes. According to Quranic teachings, every home must serve as a training centre for civic responsibilities and every home must supply society with better members. The home, in effect, is a school and husbands and wives are the teachers in that school. As good teachers they produce healthy homes and this in turn makes for make a healthy society. In this sense, a husband and a wife are the builders of a society. Indeed, they are the builders of a nation.

Life, to be worth living, requires a number of vital inputs, such as education, an understanding of life's moral principles and a willingness to uphold them.

It is a fact that men and women are both different in nature, but this difference is good for their respective roles, provided both learn the art of difference management. This habit will save their time and prevent them from being distracted from worthwhile pursuits. They will then be better able to play their roles in domestic and social life.

Nature has provided them with different fields of work, like intellectual progress, spiritual development, and giving assistance in establishing peace in society. This is the true role of both men and women. Moreover, this is the only criterion for a successful marriage.

A Predictable Character

According to the Quran, a true believer is one who has a predictable character. In the chapter *Al-Baqarah* (The Heifer) the Quran says:

> Virtuous are those who, despite their love for it, give away their wealth to their relatives and to orphans and the very poor, and to travellers and those who ask [for charity], and to set slaves free, and who attend to their prayers and pay the alms, and who keep their pledges when they make them, and show patience in hardship and adversity, and in times of distress. Such are the true believers; and such are the God-fearing. (2:177)

This Quranic verse tells us what kind of moral qualities a true believer has. The summing up of these qualities is that he is a predictable character. In every situation, you can believe with certainty that he will do this and he will not do that.

For example, if he promises you something in the course of his dealings with you, you can feel convinced that he will not break his word. He will certainly fulfil his promise. If you are in his neighbourhood, you can believe with certainty that he is not going to create any problems for you.

Being predictable in character is the best description of a true human being. Man is a social animal: he lives in a society and every time he is with other people he must exhibit the best human traits, the most important of which is his predictability. He must always fulfil predictions about himself and live up to the expectations of others regarding his speech and behaviour. His dealings should invariably be fair and just according to the accepted social norms.

A predictable character, in projecting a better image of your personality, has many benefits. It is the source of all kinds of social good

The quality of being predictable promotes high values in a society, such as mutual confidence, and it removes all kinds of negative feelings such as hate, intolerance and indifference. It, moreover, obviates any occasion for complaint, protest or conflict and prevents unnecessary misunderstanding, etc.

All good machines are predictable, but there is a difference between a man and a machine. A machine is a lifeless mechanism, the contrived product of technology, but man's predictable character is the outcome of his intellectual awakening, his ability to control his emotions, and the repeated demonstration of his just behaviour. On the one hand, it gives peace of mind to the person himself and on the other hand it helps promote a peaceful atmosphere in the society.

A predictable character means a self-disciplined character; it is a sign that the person who shows this kind of behaviour is a man of a high calibre. He has that admirable quality of being realistic in his approach. He is a positive thinker and free of all kinds of negative thought. Only men of predictable character can build a better society. There is no alternative to this.

The whole of nature is completely predictable. Nature will accept only those men and women who prove to be as predictable as other parts of nature.

Greater than Political Victory

People are generally obsessed with politics. They believe that their acquiring a territory and establishing political rule over it is the greatest kind of success. But, according to the Quran, peace is the *summum bonum*. While political victory is limited in its scope, the ambit of peace is unlimited. Peace is therefore greater than political rule.

In the chapter *Al-Fath* (Victory), the Quran refers to the Hudaybiyyah Agreement—a peace treaty drawn up between the Prophet and his opponents, which was finalized in the sixth year of the Hijra calendar. The Quran mentions it as a 'clear' victory (48:1)—a victory which is beyond any doubt.

Political rule is good only for rulers and it is bad for all those who are ruled. In contrast, peace has no such negative aspect.

Then in the chapter *Al-Nasr* (Help), the Quran refers to political victory over Makkah in the eighth year of the Hijra calendar. Here the Quran uses the word *fath* (victory). This difference of terminology proves that, according to the Quran, political victory is simply the superseding of opponents in control of a particular area, whereas establishing peace—a 'clear' victory—is the greater victory. It means that establishing peace has more importance than a political victory.

Why is there this difference? The reason is that political victory gives you only one thing and that is administrative control over a piece of land. But peace has much greater potential than this. Peace opens the door to multiple opportunities and, by availing of those opportunities, you can achieve all kinds of success, including political rule.

The early history of Islam is a clear proof of this fact. Before the peace agreement of Hudaybiyyah was signed, Islam seemed to be trapped in a blind alley. But after the Hudaybiyyah Agreement, the Prophet of Islam and his companions endeavoured to avail of all those opportunities that had been opened up to them and, within two years, Islam had spread all over the Arabian peninsula.

This principle covers all human life—family life, social life, as well as international life; everywhere you can see the miracle of this master formula. The whole of history testifies to the fact that no one has ever been able to achieve any meaningful target through political victory. On the contrary, all great achievements have been the result of peaceful activities.

Political rule has so many negative points. It leads to reaction, jealousy, enmity, even fighting and ultimately war. Political rule means one's domination over others, so every political regime, every political rule results in permanent rivalry, sometimes in the heart and sometime on the battlefield.

Political rule is good only for rulers and it is bad for all those who are ruled. In contrast, peace has no such negative aspect. Peace creates normalcy; peace promotes healthy activities, peace results in the culture of friendship. In an atmosphere of peace, all the members of a society feel that they are living in state of equality. All men and women are equal members of a large family.

People living under political rule feel that they are under someone or under some group. They are like subjects. But those who live in a peaceful atmosphere feel, consciously or unconsciously, that they are living under the universal laws of nature. No one is superior and no one is inferior. Everyone's dignity is acknowledged and maintained.

Faith is a Discovery

*I*n the chapter *Al-Ma'idah* (The Table) of the Quran, the
story is told of a group who came to the Prophet and accepted
him as a prophet:

> When they listen to what has been sent down to the
> Messenger, you see their eyes overflowing with tears,
> because of the Truth they realized. They say, 'Our
> Lord, we believe, so count us among those who bear
> witness. (5:83)

According to this verse, these people accepted the Prophet's
faith. But their acceptance was not of a simple kind: it was the
outcome of *marefat*, that is, realization of the truth.

What is realization or discovery? It is the result of deep
contemplation. When anyone ponders over nature and thinks
about himself, he discovers that there is a great mind behind this
creation. His study, his observation and contemplation, all lead
him to believe that there is this great reality. After this realization,
he feels that he has no option but to proclaim the existence of
God. The next step is to aver there is no God but the one God.

This declaration inevitably follows surrender before God.
One who makes such a declaration not only accepts the truth
but he becomes a worshipper of God and a follower of God's
guidance. His thinking, his speech, his behaviour are all coloured
in the dye of God. He adopts a God-oriented life. This faith, or
iman, revolutionizes one's thinking. It brings about a sea-change
in one's life.

Faith, or *iman*, is like a seed. A seed is a growing thing. It grows
and grows till it becomes a big tree, with roots, trunk, branches,

leaves, flowers and fruits. All these are potential parts of the seed. A tree is an actualization of a seed's potential.

The same is true of faith, or iman. Faith is like a spiritual seed. When the seed is implanted in a personality, it starts growing. There is everything in this spiritual seed, but everything is the form of potential. When it finds its place in one's mind, it starts growing and all those things that are part of the divine religion begin to unfold. This process continues till the individual becomes a divine person in the fullest sense of the word.

Faith, or iman, revolutionizes one's thinking. It brings about a sea-change in one's life.

Although faith, or *iman*, is full of potential, it does not grow automatically like the seed of a tree. It requires great endeavour and anyone who wants his personality to grow, must start an ideological struggle. Without this, no one can grow into a full-fledged tree of the divine religion.

An ideological struggle means contemplation, introspection, observation, and developing the ability to draw lessons from different kinds of experiences, accompanied, of course by a study of divine literature. All these processes are paths to spiritual development and when one follows this course he surely will reach his destination. The growth of a tree is controlled by the external laws of physics, but the growth of a divine personality is a self-controlled phenomenon.

Freedom and Determinism

The Quran sets forth the concept that God Almighty is the Lord of the Universe; He is the Sustainer and the Controller of the whole world. Man cannot do anything without God's permission (76:30).

These Quranic verses lay emphasis on the supremacy of God Almighty.

But this does not mean that in this world everything is pre-determined and man has no choice of his own.

Everyone enjoys freedom and everyone is living with his or her freedom. The way one feels about what one does, or chooses not to do, is in itself testimony to there being no compulsion; everyone does as he or she pleases. In the light of one's own experience, one feels oneself to be a free person. Human beings do, in fact, enjoy complete freedom, but this freedom is a matter of their own sense of free-will. It is everyone's own feeling or experience that he or she is not living under any compulsion or constraints.

Then what is the equation between man and God? In this world everything was created by God, and if man wants to do anything, he needs many or all of the components of the human life support system, such as sunlight, water, air, minerals, oxygen, etc. All these things are part of the earthly infrastructure and this infrastructure is under the total control of God. So, while freedom of choice is man's privilege, the required infrastructure is provided by God.

So, it is a fifty-fifty situation. Man has every right to think or plan but, when he tries to execute his planning, he has no other option than to use the divine infrastructure. In terms of free-will, he enjoys complete freedom, but in terms of infrastructure, he is completely under God's command.

There are three categories of Muslim scholars, each of whom thinks differently on this subject—*Qadriya*, *Jabriya* and *Wasatiya*. *Wasatiya* scholars believe in the above equation, that is, in terms of intention and planning, man is completely free, but in terms of implementation or actualization, man has no freedom. He is compelled to find support from God.

According to the Quran, man is accountable before God. This means that this accountability is confined to his intention or free-will. His reward or punishment will be commensurate with his intention and his right or wrong exercise of free will.

The above equation is a completely rational one. Man enjoys free-will in the complete sense of the word, but he has no power to create an infrastructure such as the life-support system or any of the other things needed for the execution of his plans. So, God Almighty has provided him with everything that is required in a good infrastructure. Man has total liberty to exercise his free-will in exploiting this infrastructure and, in doing so, experiences no restriction whatsoever.

Man's every action is being recorded by the angels of God and according to this record, a person will be either rewarded or punished on the Day of Judgement. As regards man's accountability, only one criterion will apply: whether man exercised his freedom in a proper manner or he misused his freedom.

Don't Live in Suspicion

One of the divine commandments given in the Quran is that of avoiding suspicion. In the chapter *Al-Hujurat* (The Apartments), the Quran gives important guidance:

> Believers, avoid much suspicion. Indeed, some suspicion is a sin. (49:12)

Suspicion means believing something to be bad without there being any substantial evidence. Allowing suspicion to become a habit can have a disastrous effect on any society. In moral terms, suspicion is a sin and in the legal sense it is a crime. In both cases, it is to be completely avoided.

The habit of suspicion is like smoking. It not only ruins the health of the individual who has this bad habit, but it also pollutes the whole of the social atmosphere.

The Prophet once said: "Do not be suspicious of your fellow men. Suspicion is tantamount to a lie." When you suspect another person of some wrongdoing and you have no irrefutable evidence in support of your suspicion, you are committing falsehood. In other words, you are telling a lie.

It is said that man is a social animal. Collective living is must for mankind in this world. And collective living is always based on mutual trust. Without mutual trust, no healthy society can be established. In a society where people are subject to misgivings and everyone becomes suspicious of everyone else, there can be no mutual trust.

The habit of suspicion is like smoking. It not only ruins the health of the individual who has this bad habit, but it also pollutes the whole of the social atmosphere. Suspicion is just like moral pollution. Just as air pollution is harmful for everyone so also is this kind of moral pollution. It is, in fact, like a spiritual pollution.

All those living in a society where the majority of its members are of a suspicious cast of mind, are bound to inhale its morally polluted air. Everyone is bound to suffer from bad health in terms of morality. So, suspicion is not an individual, but rather a social evil.

In such a society, everyone becomes unpredictable, causing mutual trust to disappear. And an absence of mutual trust leads to many other problems. For example, in such a society, no one will dare to support any other person and then there can be no development of the culture of friendship.

There will be no unity and solidarity in such a society. This being so, its members will lose their self-confidence and will not venture to launch any large-scale project. This is because such projects need collective efforts and collective efforts are not possible in a society where people live in an atmosphere of suspicion.

Suspicion is not a single evil; it leads to many other evils. Suspicion is like a poisonous weed which rapidly multiplies in a jungle of moral evils. Suspicion has no plus points. On all counts it has only negative points. Anyone who wants to inculcate sound thinking in his mind must avoid suspicion at all costs.

When the individual develops the habit of suspicion, it gradually becomes his second nature. He starts suspecting everything, he loses conviction and he feels that every man and woman except himself is a suspicious person. He does not realize that suspicion is the result of confused thinking and that having a suspicious nature is very dangerous for himself as well as for other individuals.

Suspicion is a kind of confusion and confusion is like poison to the mind. It is quite in order to form opinions about others, but it is completely wrong to form opinions about others based on suspicion.

Waiting for a Better Future

One of the important teachings of Islam is *sabr*, that is, patience. Patience is the key to all success. In the chapter *Al-Baqarah* (The Heifer), the Quran has this to say:

> You who believe, seek help through patience and prayer; surely, God is with the people of patience. (2:153)

Sabr, or patience, is neither a passive attitude nor any kind of inaction. According to the Quran, *sabr*, or patience, is superior action. When things are not to your liking, being patient is the equivalent of waiting for a better situation to materialize. When an unwanted situation arises and you refrain from reaction, you are simply allowing things to take their natural course. So patience is like a strategy. One could even call it a master strategy.

Our social sphere has many different elements, many of which, of their own, can lead to positive results, so if you take some abrupt action, you are not allowing time for such elements to come to your support. But when you keep your patience, it means that you are allowing all natural factors to contribute to your success.

For example, if you find yourself in the darkness of night and you start crying about this darkness, you will be wasting your energy, for this kind of crying is not going to yield any positive result. But if you simply adopt the policy of waiting, then very soon morning will come and the whole atmosphere will brighten up.

Being patient does not mean not taking any action. It means planning your strategy, assessing your resources and taking into consideration the relevant natural factors. That is right planning.

In this world, planning takes care of fifty percent of the task, while natural factors take care of the other fifty percent. They are like the two wheels of the bicycle which revolve in perfect unison to carry the cyclist to his destination. Either one without the other would only bring about chaos and catastrophe.

Being patient does not mean not taking any action. It means planning your strategy, assessing your resources and taking into consideration the relevant natural factors. That is right planning.

Patience means wisdom-based thinking. If impatience is the result of unwise thinking, patience is the result of wise thinking. That is the secret of life and also the secret of wise planning.

You cannot fight against nature, so you cannot afford the luxury of being impatient. Impatience means trying to achieve things on a unilateral basis. But that is impossible. On the other hand, having patience means doing things on a bilateral basis. And it is a fact that, in our world, unilateralism is an unrealistic approach, while bilateralism is entirely a wise approach.

The policy of wait and see is the best policy in this world, and it is this policy that is called patience. Impatience means: Don't wait, but jump into the situation without thinking about the consequences. The wait and see policy is the only wise policy in this world of competition and challenge.

Every goal needs wise planning, for it is wise planning that leads to real success. And wise planning is that in which considerations other than your emotions have been taken into account.

Wish Well, Be Honest

In the chapter *Al-A'raf* (The Heights) of the Quran, it is mentioned that when the Prophet was assigned the duty of prophethood, he came to his community and said:

> I am conveying my Lord's messages to you and I am your well-wisher and your honest adviser. (7:68)

The Prophet said this in the context of his divine mission. But this declaration also has a greater application in that it gives us two basic principles upon which to build a healthy society, that is, well-wishing and honesty. If you want to have a better society, these two principles should be adhered to, for there is no better formula for social re-engineering than the inculcation of the spirit of well-wishing and honesty in all members of society. When the majority of the individuals making up society possess these qualities, that is the best guarantee of a better society.

What is well-wishing? Well-wishing means that every member of a society is free of hatred for others, and is able to remain detached from the bad experiences which are the fault of others. He is able to love other members of society in spite of grievances.

Grievance is an unavoidable part of social life, so a member of society can wish others well only when he is able to downplay his grievances sufficiently to be able to maintain good relations with other members of his society.

What is honesty? An honest person is one who is a trustworthy person. This quality is also vital to the betterment of social living. The best society is one whose members are entirely trustworthy and responsible.

Trustworthy individuals make trustworthy societies, and trustworthy societies make trustworthy nations, and trustworthy nations provide the basis for better international relationships.

The criterion of well-wishing and honesty has a two-fold impact. On the one hand, it is the only source of individual development; it reflects the best individual character. Individuals for their own benefit need many qualities, but the essence of all these qualities can be summed up in these two words: well-wishing and honesty.

The other aspect of these two qualities is that they are the sole basis on which a better society may be built. This is the only right starting point, if you wish to have a better society. Start the process from the individual character, try to condition individuals along the lines of well-wishing and honesty, and you will find that on the culmination of the process, you will have reached your social goal.

Trustworthy individuals make trustworthy societies, and trustworthy societies make trustworthy nations, and trustworthy nations provide the basis for better international relationships.

Well-wishing and honesty are both positive qualities. If negative thinking is the source of all evil, positive thinking is the source of all kinds of goodness. So, well-wishing and honesty are not just two qualities: they include more than two thousand qualities. One who has the qualities of well-wishing and honesty will certainly possess all kinds of other good qualities.

Well-wishing and honesty are two pillars of character building and it is on these two pillars that the whole edifice of social uplift can be founded. If these pillars are weak, the whole structure will prove to be weak, but if these two pillars are strong, the whole structure will have everlasting strength.

The Quran: A Book of Contemplation

he Quran is the Book of God, revealed to the Prophet of Islam in the first quarter of the seventh century. The Quran is not a mysterious blessing; it is a book of wisdom. In the chapter *Sad* (Sad), the Quran says of itself:

> This is a blessed Book which We sent down to you [Muhammad], for people to ponder over its messages, and for those with understanding to take heed. (38:29)

The Quran is, indeed, a book of wisdom, which gives us knowledge about the divine scheme along with all those principles that are required for successful living in this world. In short, the Quran is a book of guidance for mankind. It is, moreover, a simple book, which is easily understandable to anyone who has even the most rudimentary knowledge of Arabic. But all the things it has to offer can be discovered only through contemplation. It is contemplation, or *tadabbur*, that opens the doors of the Quranic treasure of knowledge. Then the Quran is marked by the most perfect clarity, but that does not mean that you can understand the Quran without pondering over it. In fact there are two layers of Quranic learning: one, its literal meaning and the second is its deeper meaning. If you want to know the message of the Quran in a simple manner, then knowing its literal meaning will suffice.

Its literal meaning will introduce you to the basic, practical advice offered by the Quran. This kind of knowledge is quite enough for the common people who are not of a scholastic bent of mind. Then there is the deeper side of Quranic meaning. This can be comprehended only after an in-depth study of the scriptures.

The Quran is evidently a book of guidance for both the common man as well as for highly educated people. And both are equally important, there is no doubt about it. Human societies consist of both the educated and the uneducated, so it is but natural that God Almighty should send a book that would be both accessible and meaningful to both categories of people. Take the first verse of the Quran:

"All praise is due to God, the Lord of the Universe." (1:2)

This verse provides intellectual food for the common man as well as for those who have acquired great learning. Both can find spiritual nourishment in this Quranic verse.

The Quran is, indeed, a book of wisdom, which gives us knowledge about the divine scheme along with all those principles that are required for successful living in this world.

The common man will take it in its simplest sense. He will take it in the sense that he himself and the world all around him were created by God Almighty alone. So, He alone is praiseworthy, He alone deserves his gratitude.

But those who have studied the scientific disciplines, and gained knowledge of biology, physiology, physics, chemistry, geology, astronomy, etc., will take what the Quran has to say in a more profound sense. They will say that the whole world, including themselves, is a phenomenon of a highly complex creation. And, by taking into consideration all modern scientific discoveries, they will have the enthralling experience of understanding God's creation plan.

If the common man's response to this verse is his unquestioning acknowledgement of God, the educated man's response will be an even more carefully reasoned and elevated acknowledgement of his Maker.

The Human Personality

he chapter *Al-Tin* (The Fig) of the Quran is a description of the human personality. It is a relatively short chapter of just eight verses, but it has a great lesson. The translation of this chapter is as follows:

> The Fig is a witness and the Olive is a witness, and Mount Sinai is a witness, and this secure land is a witness that We have indeed created man in the best of moulds, then We cast him down as the lowest of the low, except for those who believe and do good deeds—theirs shall be an unending reward! What then after this, can make you deny the Last Judgement? Is not God the greatest of the judges? (95:1-8)

According to this chapter, man has two quite opposite futures. On the one hand, he is doomed to utter failure and on the other hand he will be rewarded with the best eternal reward. One section of humanity will have the worst fate, while another section of humanity will have the best possible fate.

In fact, God has created man with great potential and, at the same time, He has given him complete freedom of choice. It is this freedom that divides people into two categories—those who misuse their freedom and the others who use it properly.

165

The potential that man has, is bestowed directly by the Creator, but it is the duty of man himself to turn this potential into a reality. Herein lies the destiny of man. People, then, are necessarily of two categories: firstly, the failures and secondly, the successful ones.

Some achievers are said to be self-made men but, according to the divine scheme described in the Quran, everyone is a self-made man. In terms of potential, everyone is born to become a self-made man. It means that the principles of destiny are laid down by God Almighty but the making of human destiny is in the hands of every man and woman.

The crux of this divine scheme is that man should apply his reason and common sense, he should follow his conscience, he should discover the laws of nature.

Man was given freedom by his Creator. This is a great divine blessing for man. As a matter of fact, it is God Almighty alone who can dispense the good things of life. He is the only giver being in this universe. But God Almighty wanted to bestow His blessing on man as a form of credit rather than as a unilateral blessing.

The human personality is a unique phenomenon in the universe. No creature, material or non-material, has this gift of freedom of choice that man has. This gives man the highest status in the whole universe. Man must have a correct understanding of this exceptional privilege and use it properly. With its proper use a man becomes a superman, but one who misuses the opportunities opened up by freedom will be reduced to a level lower than that of the animals.

The crux of this divine scheme is that man should apply his reason and common sense, he should follow his conscience, he should discover the laws of nature, he should study the divine scriptures revealed to the prophets, he should try to find out his purpose in life and God Almighty's design regarding his creation. After taking into account all these facts, he should build his future.

Successful Leadership

Successful leadership depends on a successful following; if the followers fail to follow, no leader can play a successful role. The chapter *Al-Nisa'* (Women) of the Quran sets forth this principle:

> By your Lord, they will not be true believers until they seek your arbitration in their disputes and find within themselves no doubt about what you decide and accept it wholeheartedly. (4:65)

This Quranic verse relates to religious leadership, but the same principle is likewise applicable to the case of secular leadership. Secular leadership and religious leadership are different in their goals, but the method of both is one and the same.

Men and women are born with differences. Everyone is Mr. Different or Ms. Different, and this being so, it is not always possible to convince everyone of the correctness of the leader's decisions. It is but natural that if some members of the group are in agreement with his decisions some other members may disagree with them. This kind of difference is a natural phenomenon which occurs in both secular groups and religious groups.

Then how to establish unity? Unity is a must for a leader to be successful. Without unity among his followers a leader cannot play an effective role. In such a situation the only formula that is applicable is—follow your leader, be it willingly or unwillingly.

This is the only practical way to achieve unity: this is the sole basis for the success of the leader.

The true leader is born and not made. His principal quality is his decision-making ability. In this he is aided by his foresight, unwavering determination and his capacity for organization. Another major virtue is his lack of any desire for personal glorification. He is a man of vision, a man of integrity with no private agenda. All these qualities make for a successful leader. Any such leader will have a good reputation among his people.

But these qualities in themselves are not sufficient to ensure a successful leadership. Successful leadership depends fifty per cent upon the leader and fifty per cent upon his followers. Without a combination of the two, no leader can function successfully in either the secular or the religious sphere.

The true leader is born and not made. His principal quality is his decision-making ability. In this he is aided by his foresight, unwavering determination and his capacity for organization.

A successful leader needs material power, but power by itself does not guarantee the success of a leader. People must be aware of the benefits of unity and the pitfalls of disunity. They must bear in mind the maxim: United we stand, divided we fall.

One difference between a successful leader and an unsuccessful leader is that the former knows his followers as well as he knows himself, while the latter is one who knows himself but has no knowledge of his followers. Without having a good understanding of his followers, no leader can prove to be successful.

It is said that a successful leader is one who is also a successful pleader. Often there are occasions when you have to induce people to follow you, but there are also sometimes circumstances in which it is better to follow others. It is an appreciation of this fact that contributes to the success of the leader.

Learning Lessons

One of the major concerns of the Quran is to inculcate in every man and woman the spirit of contemplation. In the chapter *Al-Hijr* (The Rocky Tract) the Quran refers to certain historical phenomena and then says:

> There are certainly signs in that for those who can learn a lesson. (15:75)

Natural phenomena as well as historical events have great lessons for those who go deeply into them and learn lessons from them. The Quran, in referring to them, attempts to develop the thinking habit, so that readers may gain from them intellectually.

Jesus Christ once said: "Man does not live by bread alone." (Matthew 4:4) This is an important teaching of all religions. This means that all men and women need two kinds of nourishment: the physical and the spiritual. Everyone knows the importance of physical nourishment but, where spiritual nourishment is concerned, people remain in ignorance of how vital it is.

Man cannot afford to live in a state of physical starvation, for physical starvation brings on weakness and disease. Everyone, being aware of how debilitating this can be, makes sure that he or she has proper sustenance.

The same is true of spiritual starvation. Spiritual starvation makes you a weak personality. It erodes the faculty of wisdom. It deprives you of moral values. Spiritual starvation may go to such an extreme that one may face spiritual death.

To keep spirituality alive, spiritual food is at all times a necessity.

The source of that spiritual food is thinking or contemplation. Moreover, one should develop the habit of not taking things at face value. The deeper aspect of things must be gone into so that their inner meaning may be discovered. This requires an uninterrupted intellectual process.

The individual must keep his mind alive every day and every night. When he studies a book, when he observes a scene, when he is confronted by a historical event, he must properly activate his mental faculties in order to learn some spiritual lesson from it. He must endeavour to turn his experiences into meaningful lessons.

Men and animals both have experiences of different kinds each day and night, but the difference is that animals take them at face value and are unaware of the need to discover their deeper meaning.

To keep spirituality alive, spiritual food is at all times a necessity. The source of that spiritual food is thinking or contemplation.

But man has the capacity for what is called 'conceptual thought'. Man can penetrate to the deeper aspect of things, and then learn from them hidden lessons. This difference is very important. Those who fail to take lessons from experience, be they men or women, are reducing themselves to the level of animals.

Spirituality is a requirement of man: animals have no such requirement. Animals can live without spirituality, but man cannot. Man cannot afford to deprive himself of spirituality. It is in man's own interests to keep his mind alive, so that he may not lose any opportunity to learn spiritual lessons from the happenings of life.

Spirituality makes you a creative thinker: without creativity, man is little better than a stone statue.

Character Assassination

*D*uring the Prophet's time, there were certain people in Madinah who wanted to defame a member of the Prophet's family. It was a case of character assassination. At that juncture some verses were revealed in the Quran, which appear in the chapter *Al-Nur* (Light). The translation of one of these verses is quoted below:

> Those who desire that indecencies should spread among the believers, will have a painful chastisement in this world and the Hereafter. God knows, and you do not know. (24:19)

According to Islamic teachings, character assassination is a heinous crime. An act of this kind is against humanity, against ethical values, and against Quranic teachings. Those guilty of any ethical crime of this nature will be severely punished by God Almighty.

If you criticize someone on the basis of undeniable facts which stand up to objective scrutiny, you are acting lawfully and are exercising your moral rights as set forth in the divine book. If your intention is good, your action will be treated as promoting reform. Moreover, you will receive reward from God Almighty.

But if you are abusing someone, or using unethical or immoral language without any evidence to support what you say, then you are committing a crime. The use of abusive language against anyone, which has no factual base, is an act of character assassination. No one has the right to use such language.

Criticism based on facts is constructive, but making allegations without any basis in fact is the worst kind of crime.

In this regard, two courses are open to all: if an individual has an accusation to make against anyone and he has undeniable proof in support of what he has to say, then he is allowed to express his views. If, on the other hand, he has an adverse opinion about anyone, but has no evidence to support his negative remarks, then he has to remain silent. No one is allowed to make damaging remarks against anyone if he cannot produce irrefutable proofs of the truth of his statement.

The Prophet once said: "If you make a negative remark against someone while that person is innocent, then it will have a boomerang effect. Your negative remark will turn back upon you and you will find that remark being applied to you." (*Sahih al-Bukhari*, 6045)

According to Islamic teachings, character assassination is a heinous crime. An act of this kind is against humanity, against ethical values.

The practice of character assassination is injurious to the whole of society; it spreads the feeling of mistrust. It causes misunderstanding and the result is very dangerous, for everyone becomes suspicious of the other members of society.

In such a society, no healthy activity is possible and no positive planning can be done. The habit of character assassination is bad for all and good for none.

The whole of society must be alert to anyone indulging in this kind of activity and the wrongdoer must be openly condemned. Indeed, social ostracism is the only check by which this kind of baneful habit can be eliminated from society.

Character assassination is more dangerous than physical

assassination. Any society that ignores this heinous practice is callous and inhuman.

A Sense of Accountability

One of the important teachings of Islam is the concept of accountability. According to the Quran, life is a very serious business, for which reason everyone ought to be imbued with a total sense of accountability. In the chapter *Al-Isra'* (The Night Journey) of the Quran, this concept is gone into in detail:

> Give full measure, when you measure, and weigh with accurate scales. That is fair, and better in the end. Do not follow what you do not know; for the ear and the eye and the heart shall all be called to account. (17:35-36)

Everything we say is inevitably based on information that we gather from outside. Basically, there are three sources: what we hear, what we see, and what we think. These three senses give us what may be called data, but in each case there is the possibility of misunderstanding or miscalculation, so we have to be very careful to be precise in all of our utterances.

The expressions in the above verse concerning weights and measures are used symbolically. Here, measuring or weighing means intellectual measuring or intellectual weighing. We should be very accurate when we speak about anyone or about any issue. Our behaviour must be as precise as a scientific scale.

Right thinking and precise speaking are moral requirements: neglect of these matters can have very serious consequences. Since everything is known to God Almighty, everyone will be punished or rewarded according to how he speaks and behaves.

This being so, every man or woman must of necessity be very serious. In the firm belief that one day he will be presented before the all-knowing God, everyone must conduct himself with a deep sense of responsibility.

Everyone will face an unavoidable judgement issued by God Almighty. This Quranic teaching is very important, for it provides a great incentive to the building of a person as a righteous and healthy member of society.

Experience shows that sermons alone cannot suffice. No sermon, however powerful, can change people; every good sermon needs one more thing: fear of punishment. It is only fear of punishment that guarantees that people will develop the right kind of character.

Right thinking and precise speaking are moral requirements: neglect of these matters can have very serious consequences.

If you deliver sermons, people will find some excuse not to follow their teachings. It is only the fear of punishment that will make the content of those sermons of immediate personal interest. Such fear inculcates the right spirit. Even if you have a good excuse for wrong behaviour, don't use it. Because if you use it, you shall have to pay a heavy price and the law is the law: it brooks no excuses.

Living in fear of punishment is not a negative feeling. It is a completely positive feeling. It turns you into a responsible person; it inculcates the spirit of self-discipline. It makes you an honest person, building into your personality a welcome predictability. And it saves you from all kinds of deviation.

A sense of accountability makes you manage your affairs in the best possible way. It compels you to make the best use of your time, energy and resources.

The Role of a Woman

According to Quranic as well as Biblical accounts, Moses was born into an Israelite family. The Egyptian king, Pharaoh, had ordered all the Israelite boys to be killed as soon as they were born. But God Almighty intervened and made Moses the exception. One part of his story is given in the chapter *Al-Qasas* (The Story) of the Quran:

> We inspired Moses' mother saying, 'Suckle him, and then, when you fear for him, cast him into the river, and have no fear and do not grieve, for We shall return him to you, and shall make him one of the Messengers.' Then Pharaoh's household picked him up—later to become for them an enemy and a source of grief for them: Pharaoh and Haman and their hosts were wrongdoers—and Pharaoh's wife said, 'He will be a joy to the eye for me and you! Do not slay him: he may well be of use to us, or we may adopt him as a son.' They did not realize what they were doing. Moses' mother's heart was full of anxiety—she would have disclosed his identity had We not strengthened her heart so that she might be a firm believer [in Our promise]. She said to Moses' sister, 'Go, and follow him.' So she watched him from a distance, like a stranger, without anyone noticing her. We had already made him refuse all wet nurses. So his sister said to them, 'Shall I tell you of a family who will bring him up for you and take good care of him?' Thus We restored him to his mother, so that she might be comforted and not grieve any more, and so that she would know

that God's promise was true. But most of them do not realize this. (28:7-13)

This part of Moses' story gives us an interesting example of how a woman can play an important role. Moses' sister, Mariam, just fifteen years old at the time, was able to enter Pharaoh's palace—where it would have been impossible for a man to go. It was possibly because of her youth and femininity that she was able to do so. From this it would appear that sometimes a woman can play a more subtle role than a man. And the above incident gives a very fine example of this reality.

According to the Quran, men and women are born different from each other in nature. The Quran holds that men and women are both equal in the sense of being worthy of respect, but that they are different in the roles they play.

Men can perform certain tasks better than women, and at the same time, women can perform certain tasks better than men. This is according to the creation plan of God. The Quran propounds the equality of men and women as human beings, but does not apply this rule for every kind of task to be undertaken. The above-mentioned story provides a good example of this.

The Quran holds that men and women are both equal in the sense of being worthy of respect, but that they are different in the roles they play.

Human life has different aspects; it requires different abilities for different kinds of undertakings in every walk of life. That is why God Almighty created men and women with different qualities. This difference is exactly in consonance with specific needs. A good human life can be built only by accepting this reality of creation.

Speech Management

One of the important teachings of the Quran is what may be called 'speech management'. That is, the use of words with an extreme sense of responsibility and not letting one's tongue get out of control. This teaching is stressed in the chapter *Al-Nisa'* (Women) of the Quran:

> There is no good in most of their secret talk, except in the case of those who enjoin charity and kindness, or reconciliation between people. If anyone does that, seeking the pleasure of God, We will give him an immense reward. (4:114)

This Quranic verse does not pertain to specifically secret talk. It includes all kinds of talks and conversations. The power of speech given to man is a very rare quality. It is an exclusive boon for both men and women. But, every gift involves responsibility, and this is especially true in the case of the power of speech. One must use this power with great caution.

Speech, to be of proper value, must be used in those fields which are useful for mankind. Such use of speech is worthy of reward, while the misuse of speech is liable to punishment.

The art of speech management means the control of your tongue, thinking before speaking and calculating in advance the impact of what you have to say.

You should avoid negative talk, telling lies, misrepresentation of facts and any kind of utterances which may create a rift or suspicion between two people or two groups. Speech is most commonly misused when people do not know the difference between an allegation and a statement based on evidence.

If you want to say anything about anyone, first of all you have to examine whether what you have to say is supported by logic or not. If you have good reason to speak, then you may open your mouth, otherwise you should remain silent. Here the options are clear.

What is right speech? Right speech is that which is based on truth, which will stand up to objective analysis—being based on certified data which is positive in nature—and which will not create any unnecessary problems.

All human activities are related to speech in some way or the other. So, every man and woman must develop the art of speaking in a manner which is positive and which creates a healthy atmosphere in all important spheres—the family, society and the nation. Good speech is the basis of nation building.

The art of speech management means the control of your tongue, thinking before speaking and calculating in advance the impact of what you have to say.

People generally live without discipline; they dislike imposing any constraints on their activities. This is very true of speech. Right speech means disciplined speech, talking in a properly controlled way. That is, weighing every word before speaking. Futile speech is good for nothing, whereas well-considered speech is a source of the greatest good.

The art of speech management is the most vital art for a man or a woman. Without acquiring this art, a man is only half a man and a woman is only half a woman. Only those—both men and women—who have developed the art of right speech, can be said to be complete human beings.

Don't be a Slave to Your Desires

*D*esires are an integral part of human nature. All men and women have a strong tilt towards fulfilling their desires and this is their greatest weakness. Pointing out the gravity of this failing, the chapter *Al-Jathiyah* (Kneeling) of the Quran admonishes us on this subject in alarming terms:

> Consider the one who has taken his own desire as a deity, whom God allows to stray in the face of knowledge, sealing his ears and heart and covering his eyes—who can guide such a person after God [has abandoned him]? Will you not take heed? (45:23)

Desire is an essential part of one's personality. But it is like grease to an engine and not like the driver of that engine. Desire can serve as a motive force, but mindless yielding to desire will lead to disaster. If you want to be successful, try to steer your life in a rational manner. Don't give it over to your desires. Remember that where desire is blind, reason has the capacity to discern the true nature of things.

It is said that man is a slave to desire. But this saying expresses only half of the truth. It is a fact that the human mind is full of desires but, at the same time, it is also true that man's mind has the capacity for logical thought.

When you find that your mind is overwhelmed by desire, examine that desire in the light of reality. Assess it in terms of its potential results, and find out objectively whether it is feasible or not to fulfil it. Judge it by all the possible effects it can have, whether good or bad. Then, after a complete examination, if you are satisfied that its results will be beneficial, go ahead and fulfil your desire—but with great care and planning.

Don't run after your desires. Even if you are following your desires, check and re-check them again and again. Don't wait for the end result, but keep evaluating and re-evaluating them as you go along. It is also very important to turn back if you find that you have taken a wrong step. Stop your journey before reaching the point of no return.

Right desires are helpful for the development of your character. But bad desires are detrimental to your personality.

Then there are different kinds of desires, some of which are improper. You have to distance yourself from desires of this kind. Other desires are quite proper and you may entertain them. But always keep this fact in mind that every desire must remain within certain boundaries. Even good desires are useful only in a limited manner.

Right desires are helpful for the development of your character. But bad desires are detrimental to your personality. If you follow your bad desires, they can ruin your future to the extent that you cannot ever recover from their effects. You must therefore live a life that is reason-based and not desire-based.

Never judge a desire for its own sake: always judge it in terms of the result of its fulfilment. This result is the only criterion by which it may be determined whether a desire is good or bad for your life. Desire cannot be eliminated, but it can certainly be controlled. Don't become a victim of your desires. Prove to be well in control of your desires.

The Money Culture

*R*elative to money, there are two cultures prevailing in our society—money for the sake of man and man for the sake of money. The Quran rejects the concept of man for the sake of money, subscribing to the other concept that money is for the sake of man. In the chapter *Al-Takathur* (Greed for More and More) the Quran has this to say:

You were obsessed by greed for more and more till you reached the grave. (102: 1-2)

According to the Quranic concept, money or material goods are only meant to fulfil man's needs. Money is not a goal in itself. Money can fulfil the physical requirements of man, but man is more than a physical entity. Man is an intellectual being, and as such can find fulfilment in pursuing some alternative goal which is higher than that of money.

What is that higher goal for a man? It is intellectual development; it is to unfold the spiritual nature of his personality; it is to enhance his mental capacity. All these things are superior to man's physical being.

When man takes money as something which will fulfil his needs, he remains on the right path. He can travel along the road of life smoothly and successfully. But when he takes money as his supreme goal, he goes astray. For both men and women money-oriented thinking is the greatest source of distraction from the right path.

Man is greater than money. Man should live for a higher purpose and he should use money solely as his material base for constructive activity. Money is certainly useful for man, but it is certainly a wrong option if he focuses on the acquisition and hoarding of money as the principal ends in his life.

Money gives you material comfort, but it cannot give you wisdom and learning. The best course is for you to live as a seeker of truth, wisdom, learning and ultimately a goal that is elevated. That is the only right way of life for man.

It is true that money does effectively render material assistance. In that sense, it is a good helper. But it is not a good leader. A money-obsessed man is like one who has made money his leader. Money which is commensurate with needs is good, but excess money is bad. Save yourself from greed and then you will be able to save yourself from being overly money-minded.

Money gives you material comfort, but it cannot give you wisdom and learning. The best course is for you to live as a seeker of truth, wisdom, learning and ultimately a goal that is elevated.

Money is very helpful in some respects, for example, when it is used to acquire knowledge or to establish a library or a college. There are many such activities which need money. Indeed, without money it is very difficult to have a successful life on this earth.

Money has both its plus points and its minus points. One plus point of money is that it provides a good material source for worthwhile objectives, while a minus point is that its possession can be like taking an overdose of sleeping pills. And an overdose of sleeping pills sometimes kills the person who takes it.

Money for the sake of money is bad, but money for the sake of some higher purpose is good; money as a necessity is good, but the money culture per se is a disaster. The money culture reduces a man to the animal level.

Learning from Everyone

The Quran lays great importance on learning, for it is learning that promotes and sustains the process of intellectual development. A verse of the Quran in the chapter *Maryam* (Mary) gives a notable example of this in a conversation the Prophet Abraham had with his father:

> Father, I have been given some knowledge which has not come to you, so follow me: I shall guide you along a straight path. (19:43)

Obviously, Abraham's father, who was called Azar, was Abraham's senior. So he could have been reluctant to take advice from someone who was very much his junior. But in the matter of learning, senior and junior have no meaning, for words of wisdom should be heeded, even if the speaker of those words is a much younger person.

This is the true spirit of learning. Without this spirit, the learning process would be a non-starter. And without the learning process, there can be no intellectual development. If you want to be an intellectually superior person, adopt the habit of acquiring knowledge from all and sundry.

The universe of knowledge and wisdom is so vast that it cannot be encompassed by any single mind. The only thing that can help you to gain more and more knowledge is the spirit mentioned in the Quran. Everyone must develop an insatiable intellectual thirst for the gaining of knowledge from many different quarters— every day and every night.

Knowledge is like a great ocean: faced with its immensity, no one can be a self-sufficient person. The process of seeking knowledge has to be a mutual venture, in the course of which everyone gains something from everyone else. Here the taker is the giver and the giver is the taker. Everyone plays both roles.

There are several ways of acquiring knowledge, one of them being through discussion or dialogue. Discussion or dialogue is not just a debating practice; it is an intellectual exchange. Discussion, if it is to be fruitful, requires objectivity and must be carried on in the questing spirit of give and take.

Books are a great source of knowledge. But the study of books is not simply reading. It is establishing contact and consulting with other thinkers and scholars. It is like a global discussion, if the reader has the true spirit, and has the ability to acquire knowledge from universal sources. The library is the place for this, for it is like a global conference room. A library makes it possible for you to reach all the world's minds.

Discussion or dialogue is not just a debating practice; it is an intellectual exchange. Discussion, if it is to be fruitful, requires objectivity and must be carried on in the questing spirit of give and take.

The learning process is a must for everyone and that applies to both men and women. The old man is just as much in need of it as the young man. Even great scholars are no exception in this regard. One scholar has rightly said, 'Live with the spirit of learning and die with the spirit of learning.' Learning is a lifelong process. It has a beginning, but no end.

The Prophet of Islam once said that you should acquire wisdom, even if you have to go to the ends of the earth. This shows the true spirit of learning. And all men and women should become imbued with this spirit.

Six Magic Words

The Quran gives a description of how God Almighty created the universe. In one such statement the Quran, in the chapter Al-Sajdah (Prostration), tells us that God created the universe in six days:

> It was God who created the heavens and the earth and whatsoever is in between in six Days, and then He established Himself on the throne. You have no patron nor any intercessor besides Him. So will you not pay heed? (32:4)

The word 'six' in the Quran is given with reference to creation, but it also gives us an important clue for life building. This formula again comprises of six words: Ignore minus, avail of the plus.

In fact, God has created this world in such a way that it is full of possibilities. Every time you find yourself in a situation where you are facing unwanted minus points, rest assured that there will also be some plus points that are favourable to you.

So, don't despair or be disappointed, but concentrate rather on discovering those plus points. Very soon you will find that, clearly, the plus points outnumber the minus points.

Life is a test for everyone, with each problematic situation calling for reflection. Every such situation presents an intellectual challenge in that it awakens your mind and compels you to ferret out the plus items from the jungle of minus items.

Every man and woman should be made aware of nature's formula for dealing with life's problems, i.e. ascertain in advance that challenges are temporary and not permanent in nature and then try to overcome the obstacles they place in your path with wise and careful planning. You will soon discover that such challenges are only stepping stones in your life.

The minus points of life are not simply minus points. They act as a booster, they awaken your mind, they enhance your intellectual capacity, they enable you to enter into the process of struggle with greater energy and wisdom. The minus items only ensure that your success will be on a greater scale.

The minus points in life are like friction on the road. Every road is full of minor points of friction, but these only accelerate the pace of the vehicle; the same is true of human life. The problems in life can be compared to friction.

Every such situation presents an intellectual challenge in that it awakens your mind and compels you to ferret out the plus items from the jungle of minus items.

In fact, minus points and plus points are both relative terms. In real life, every minus is followed by a plus, and every plus is followed by a minus The journey of life is like travelling in a vehicle with two wheels, both of which are equally important, one wheel representing the plus points and the other wheel the minus points. You cannot run your vehicle on a single wheel; the vehicle of life needs two wheels, both minus and plus. It is one of the laws of nature, and there is no escape from the natural laws.

The formula for success comprises of only six words. Keep in mind these six words and be certain of success.

No Double Standards

*A*ccording to the Quran, it is a sign of a bad character to have double standards. Two verses of the chapter *Al-Saff* (Ranks) are of relevance:

O faithful! Why do you say one thing and do another? It is most hateful to God that you do not practise what you preach. (61:2-3)

Having double standards is anathema in this world. It is a kind of hypocrisy and hypocrisy is completely unwanted in Islam as well as in nature. A person with double standards believes himself to be a good person but, in the eyes of others, he is certainly a bad person. Double standards are alien to personal integrity. Integrity is a part of faith. One who loses his integrity will consequently lose his faith.

Double standards are a perpetual obstacle to personality development. One who habitually observes double standards will not be a strong personality. People of this kind will inevitably live with a weak personality and die with a weak personality.

Such people are devoid of sincerity. They say one thing but do something else. It is their petty interests which control their behaviour. They are not controlled by firm principles but by immediate gain. Their behaviour is interest-based rather than principle-based.

The character of those with double standards is not predictable. Such people talk much, but fail to back up their avowed resolutions with firmness of action. As a result, they will very soon lose the trust of their society. They appear to be human but, in fact, they resemble sub-human creatures.

Having double standards means saying one thing and then doing something else. This kind of character is completely alien to the world of nature. No animal shows a character of this kind. It is only man who indulges in this kind of inhuman behaviour.

Our tongues were not made for double talk. Our minds were not created for double thinking. Our personality was not made to live a life like this. One who descends to double talk and double thinking is bound to become unwanted in this world of truth. Our world is a world of truth and it is not ready to accept anything that is not based on truth.

Having double standards means being a characterless person. A man of character cannot afford this kind of duality. A man of character is a man of principle, a man of integrity. A man of character is, in short, a trustworthy person.

The character of those with double standards is not predictable. Such people talk much, but fail to back up their avowed resolutions with firmness of action.

Those flawed by such duality are unable to achieve any great success. All the super achievers of history were men of integrity. Those with double standards will lose all those qualities which are essential for super achievement. Double standards make people directionless. And one who is directionless cannot embark on a journey of any importance

People of this kind always believe that they are very clever, but they are not. The really clever person is one who can rightfully convince others to trust him. Those with double standards inevitably fail to establish goodwill or trust in society. Such people display themselves as beautiful flowers but, in fact, they are flowers of plastic, not real flowers.

Widening the Horizon

he Quran lays great emphasis on learning—through greater experience, more profound study and keener observation. In the chapter *Al-Hajj* (The Pilgrimage) of the Quran, one of the verses elaborates this point:

> Have these people not travelled through the land to make their hearts understand and let their ears hear; the truth is that it is not the eyes that are blind but the hearts that are in the bosoms that are blinded. (22:46)

Travel, which is quite in accordance with the Quranic scheme of things, is a great source of diverse experience. However, the Quran does not favour travel for entertainment but rather advises the undertaking of journeys in order to acquire knowledge and experience. Indeed, travel facilitates the study of history and an understanding of nature. In the real world, travel of this kind is highly appreciable as part of the Quranic way of life.

This does not mean that you have to travel especially for this purpose. It simply means that you have to travel keeping the spiritual and intellectual benefits of journeying in mind. Man has always been in the habit of travelling for different purposes. Moving from place to place is a part of life. But the Quran insists that when you must, travel with this mind. Whether your journey is for business or for other purposes, you have to develop that kind of eye which can see things in the light of experience and which can learn lessons from observation.

Tawassum means to elicit spiritual lessons from material experiences. And Quranic travel is that which is based on the concept of *tawassum*. For example, when you purchase a ticket from an airline office, you notice that it records your itinerary from one destination to another. Just by seeing this on your ticket, you think that some day you will be given another ticket that will be for a quite different destination, that is, from world of man to the world of God.

When you travel you have so many experiences—some good and some bad, some pleasant and some unpleasant. But there is a common aspect to all of these experiences and that is the spiritual lessons they have to offer. So, extract that kind of spiritual lesson from all your experiences, both negative and positive. If you develop this kind of habit, travel will certainly be a spiritual journey.

Travel is a great source of universal wisdom. It is a realistic means of broadening your horizons, for after every journey, you will have learnt additional lessons and will return with increased knowledge.

The mode of travel may be different—car, bus, railroad, aeroplane, or ship. But no journey is devoid of spiritual experience. So do not concern yourself with modes of travel. Always prove to be a spiritual observer, even if you are on a journey on foot. In that way, you can learn lessons perhaps even more effectively than on a journey by aeroplane.

Language should be no barrier to learning from experience. Your mother tongue may be different from that of the areas through which you pass, but you can continue to learn valuable lessons, for natural scenes or historical monuments have no special language: they speak in the language of common sense. So in all situations, you can establish contact with them and learn lessons from them.

Travel is a great source of universal wisdom. It is a realistic means of broadening your horizons, for after every journey, you will have learnt additional lessons and will return with increased knowledge. Your mind will have expanded as never before.

The Quran as a Book

The Quran appears to be a book just like any other book. But the Quran is a book with a difference. Scholars maintain that it requires almost eighty disciplines to understand the Quran, but more important than all these disciplines is sincerity. Without great sincerity, no one can understand the Quran, no on can penetrate its wisdom. No one can understand its deeper meaning.

What is sincerity? Sincerity is only another name for objectivity, without which one cannot comprehend the deeper meaning of the Quran. Most people are obsessed with different kinds of prejudices. And prejudices are the greatest hindrance to understanding the Quran. It is only if you rid your mind of them that you will be able to understand its meaning.

The Quran, relatively speaking, is a modest book and its language is also very simple. To appreciate the Quran, you don't need to understand it from A to Z. Although there is a comprehensive theme that covers all the chapters of the Quran, at the same time every single verse of the Quran has an independent meaning. One can learn some very important lessons from pondering over just a single verse. One scholar has rightly said:

"One verse a day keeps the Devil away."

The verses of the Quran total approximately six thousand three hundred. These are arranged in the form of one hundred and fourteen chapters, some long, some very short. Every chapter, except one, begins with the words: "In the name of God, the most merciful, the most compassionate." All the statements of the Quran relate to God Almighty, sometimes directly and sometimes indirectly. In the Quran, God Almighty directly addresses man saying: 'O man! This is your God addressing you. Listen to Me and follow it. This is the path of success for you.'

Some of the teachings of the Quran are eternal, such as *zikr*, that is, remembrance of God. Then there are a number of provisional teachings like *jihad*. It is very important to differentiate between the two kinds of verses. Without keeping this principle in mind, you are likely to misinterpret the scriptures. There are occasions when the Quran refers to particular events that occurred during the Prophet's lifetime, but it should be borne in mind that the themes are universal. Here, in giving a particular reference, it is the intention of the Quran to give a common message. This principle is also very important, for without keeping it in mind, no one can properly interpret the real meaning of the Quran.

'Quran' is an Arabic word. Its literal meaning is 'to be read'. This means that the Quran is a book of study.

In one sense, the Quran is a very comprehensive book, including as it does many references from history, astronomy, physical events and natural phenomena. But the majority of these references are expressed not in detail but in the form of allusions or hints. The reader must supply the details from his own knowledge and experience. Having done so, he can understand the comprehensive meaning of the Quran.

The Quran also records the history of the prophets. It refers to more than two dozen prophets of different times and different races. Every prophet was sent into different situations, and each one bore some specific message. In this sense, all the prophets are equal; every prophet is a source of guidance. One who wants to understand the prophetic mission must study all the prophets and not just any one of them at random.

'Quran' is an Arabic word. Its literal meaning is 'to be read'. This means that the Quran is a book of study. Indeed, the Quran suggests that every man and woman should read and study and explore the truth. Since study, to be successful, must be imbued with the spirit of inquiry, the message of the Quran is: Be a seeker, study, and contemplate. Analyze knowledge in an unbiased manner. And then you will reach the truth. According to the Quran, this is the *sirat-e-mustaqeem* (straight path) (1:6). One should follow this straight path and then one will certainly reach the final destination, that is, success in both the periods of life—in the pre-death period and in the post-death period.

No Pollution

Pollution of any kind is against the scheme of God the Creator. It is man's duty, therefore, to maintain the purity of nature. Failure to do so is, in religious terms, a sin and, in legal terms, a crime. Man is permitted to exploit natural resources for their benefits, but he must do so without destroying the natural order of things.

One verse worth quoting from the Quran on this subject is from the chapter Al-A'raf (The Heights); another relevant verse is from the chapter Al-'Ankabut (The Spider):

> Do not corrupt the land after it has been set in order. This is for your own good, if you are true believers (7:85)

> Corruption has appeared on land and sea because of

the evil which men's hands have done: and so He will make them taste the fruit of some of their doings, so that they may turn back from evil. (30:41)

The message of these two verses is that God Almighty has created things in their best order and man is allowed to enjoy these things for his own benefit. But he is not allowed to destroy the balance of nature. Man was born as a free creature, but man's freedom ends where his mismanagement of nature begins.

In these verses, the Quran refers to land pollution and water pollution by name but, in their general application, all kinds of pollution are included, such as air pollution, noise pollution, etc.

Man is permitted to exploit natural resources for their benefits, but he must do so without destroying the natural order of things.

Man is not the creator of this world. Man is only a beneficiary of God's creation. Man ought to be aware of this fact, for transgressing his limits will prove to be disastrous for him. All kinds of pollution are man-made, (pollution is unknown in nature; nature never created any kind of pollution) but where man has the capacity to pollute nature, he does not have the power to create another world. So, becoming sinful before God and depriving himself of the only source of life, that is, nature, is a double loss for man. This state of affairs requires man to be very careful, to be very cautious, otherwise he will be compelled to pay a very heavy price for his negligence.

Man must, of course, utilize natural bounties but he must do so with great care, because he has no alternative to the present world. The greatest minus point of human beings is that they can enjoy this world but have no power to create a new world.

What is pollution? It is the making of things impure. Things are pure by their nature; it is man who, due to his bad management, makes things impure. Man must know his limitations. Any move to pollute nature is like a suicidal act.

The most crucial aspect of this issue is that, in terms of creation, man is completely helpless; he cannot of his own create a single particle. He cannot even create a single leaf of a tree, nor can he create a single drop of water. This being the situation, man must become fully aware of his shortcomings and try to live in this world as a responsible member of society.

The Gist of the Quran

⁓⁂⁓

The first verse of the Quran tells us what the gist of the Quran is. All other parts of the Quran are only details of this first verse either directly or indirectly. It is the first verse of the chapter *Al-Fatiha*. The translation of this verse is like this:

> All praise is due to God, the Lord of the Universe (1:2)

Here the Quranic word used for praise is *hamd*. *Hamd* is a very comprehensive word in the Arabic language. It includes praise, gratefulness, and acknowledgment with a sense of awe. According to the Quran, *hamd* is a universal culture. All the creatures of the universe, living and non-living both present *hamd* toward their Creator. *Hamd* is their daily worship. Thus the whole universe acknowledges the glory of God Almighty.

Man and other creatures acknowledge the glory of God, but there is a difference, the *hamd* of the other creatures is a programmed *hamd*: it is inculcated in them by the angels of God. This fact is given the Quran:

> Do you not see that all those who are in the heavens and on earth praise God, as do the birds with wings

outstretched? Each knows his own mode of prayer and glorification: God has full knowledge of all that they do. (24:41)

But man's case is quite different. Man was born with a mind that has a unique capacity, he was given full freedom. Man does everything by his own choice. So, man's *hamd* is *hamd* by choice. Man's *hamd* is not programmed *hamd*, but his *hamd* is a self-realized *hamd*, discovered by himself. This is the dignity of man.

Material world is controlled by the law of nature. Animals behave under their instinct; all the creatures other than man, behave like computer or robots. Their hamd is no doubt a pure hamd, but in computer terms it is a programmed hamd.

All the creatures of the universe, living and non-living both present hamd toward their Creator. Hamd is their daily worship. Thus the whole universe acknowledges the glory of God Almighty.

Man is the only creature in this vast universe who enjoys complete freedom. Man possesses the thinking capacity in absolute sense of the word. Man thinks, observes, contemplates, analyzes things, thus he discovers the glory of God reflected in His creation.

After acquiring this self-discovered knowledge he exclaims: 'O God, I witness Your existence, I acknowledge Your glory, I surrender before You. You are my Lord and I am your subject.' This is the greatest *hamd* and this kind of hamd can be expressed only by human beings.

The chapter *Al-Dhariyat* (Scattering Winds) of the Quran tells us the purpose of creation in these words:

I created the jinn and mankind only so that they might worship Me: I seek no sustenance from them, nor do

I want them to feed Me—it is God who is the great Sustainer, the Mighty One, the Invincible. (51: 56-58)

According to the commentators of the Quran, here worship (*ibadat*) means *marefat*. What is *marefat?* *Marefat* means realization of God through contemplation. When one realizes God, he falls into a great sense of awe, and *hamd* is only an expression of this kind of deep feeling towards the Lord of the Universe.

From One to One Hundred Fourteen

Quran is a divine book. It was revealed to Muhammad, the Prophet, in first quarter of the seventh century. Its language is Arabic. There are in all one hundred and fourteen chapters in the Quran. The Quran is a book with a difference.

The Quran deals with almost all the issues related to mankind. Its language is very simple. Its clarity is par excellence. The first two verses of the first chapter are like this:

All praise is due to God, the Lord of the Universe, the Beneficent, the Merciful. (1:1-2)

These two verses represent the gist of the Quranic message. It means that man should acknowledge God as the Creator, as the Sustainer, and as compassionate to all His Creatures. This is the beginning of divine knowledge. This determines the right way of life for man in this world.

The last two verses of the last chapter are like this:

(I seek divine refuge from) Who whispers into the hearts of people,—among jinn and among men. (114:5-6)

The above reference from the last Quranic chapter tells us that in the present world man has to face great challenge from Satan and bad people in terms of *waswasa*.

Waswasa means misleading whisper. This is the greatest problem. Every human being lives with those evil persons who by the way of whisper always try to mislead and deviate him from the right path. Every human being, both men and women, face this challenge constantly. Man should realize this challenge and must meet this challenge with intellectual awakening and with determination.

Every human being lives between two contradictory forces. On the one hand, man is helped by God and His angels; this force is a blessing for man and it works as a positive force. It gives light and strength at every moment. Although there is no compulsion but it works as a great supporter for man.

The Quran deals with almost all the issues related to mankind. Its language is very simple. Its clarity is par excellence.

On the other hand, there are devils and also bad people who are not friendly toward man, they always try to divert his thinking from positivity to negativity, they always try to deviate man from the straight path of truth.

Both the forces work through inspiration. God and His angels inculcate positive inspiration at every occasion. They always give you the right guidance through right thinking. But the evil forces inculcate negative inspiration in your personality. They try to corrupt your intellectual process. They try to mislead by giving wrong advices at every juncture of your life.

The success of human beings in this world completely depends on this realization. One who succeeds to realize the fact that he is constantly under double forces, will prove to be successful, and one who fails to realize this fact he is doomed to failure.

The single point formula of success for every man and woman therefore can be described in one line: Be cautious. Try to establish contact with God and angels, and try to detach yourself from the evil forces of both man and Satan. Attachment and detachment are psychological processes and can be established only in the world of consciousness.

High Thinking

The chapter *Al-Ahzab* (The Confederates) of the Quran refers to what is called zikr Allah in the Quran. The translation of the relevant verse of the said chapter is as under:

Believers, remember God with much remembrance. (33:41)

God Almighty is the Creator of the Universe. God is the highest reality. God is beyond time and space. God is omnipresent. God is greater than all great things. God is supreme in every sense of the word.

Remembering God, in other words, means remembering the Higher Reality. This kind of remembrance inculcates in one's mind, high thinking and high thinking is the source of all kinds of high ideals. It is high thinking that makes one's personality a great personality. High thinking leads to spiritual uplift and intellectual development.

There are two worlds—material world and immaterial world. High thinking means thinking about the immaterial world. High thinking means living in the immaterial world. It is this immaterial world that is called the spiritual world, and it is spiritual thinking that leads to intellectual development.

Living in the immaterial world does not mean abandoning the material world and taking refuge in jungles and mountains. No, immaterial living means to extract immaterial items from the material world. When you are able to extract spiritual lessons from the material world, you are a spiritual person, that is, you have discovered the inner meaning of the external world.

Material world is full of immaterial lessons. In every material experience there are some meaningful lessons. Find out these lessons and you are spiritually a developed person.

Materialism means living in material desires like money, fame, power, etc. Immaterialism means living in goals that are higher than material goods. This kind of living inculcates high thinking, and high thinking leads to spirituality.

High thinking means living in high ideals. When you set a goal above the material goods, you are living in high thinking. High thinking is the greatest achievement in this world. High thinking is the only wealth that cannot be looted or destroyed.

Materialism means living in material desires like money, fame, power, etc. Immaterialism means living in goals that are higher than material goods. This kind of living inculcates high thinking, and high thinking leads to spirituality.

Air is a physical demonstration of high thinking. Air travels and moves around, but there is no clash or confrontation, so is the case of high thinking. A person who is a high thinker cannot waste his time in clashes and confrontations, he will set his journey beyond all these things. Nothing can stop the speed of air. So is the case of a high thinker. Nothing has the power to stop the journey of a high thinker.

A high thinker is free of all kinds of negative thought. He is free of anger and lust; he is free of intolerance and confrontation, he is free of hate, he is free of frustration and despair, he is free of tension and stress, he is free of complaint and protest.

A high thinker is free of all kinds of negativity and he is full of all kinds of positive thoughts. High thinking makes a man superman. High thinking develops the very important ability to act and not to react. Such a person is able to ignore all the problems and avail all the opportunities.

Asking the Blessing of God

*E*veryone asks blessings from God, but he or she feels that it is a unilateral blessing; I have nothing to give God in return for His blessing. In such a situation, a person faces the questions: how to ask blessings from God, how to invoke God for His blessing towards him.

When one reads the Quran with this mind, one finds a very relevant reference in the Quran. In one part of the Quran there are the details of the law of inheritance, how to apportion the bequest among relatives after the death of a family member. In this regard in chapter *Al-Nisa'* (Women) Quran says:

> If other relatives, orphans or needy people are present
> at the time of the division, then provide for them out
> of it, and speak kindly to them. (4:8)

Here God Almighty laid a principle for man to give to not only to the deserving ones but also to those persons who do not deserve. So, one can make this a point of reference for prayer. One can say in one's prayer that: 'O God, bestow on me the same mercy which You have enjoined man to bestow on man.'

It is a way of praying to use some event as a point of reference for prayer. The above verse provides us with a very important point of reference: it is impossible that God Almighty asks man to give blessing to others and that He himself is deprived of this blessing. Certainly God is in a position to bestow that kind of blessing billion times more than a man, since man was created by God.

The Prophet once said that one who asks God with the reference of *ism-e-azam* (the greatest name), his prayer will certainly be fulfilled by God. What is asking by referring to *ism-e-azam*? It is that kind of prayer which can invoke God Almighty, and the above-mentioned prayer falls in this category. If one asks God by the way of invoking His attributes, one will certainly be responded to positively.

> *Certainly God is in a position to bestow that kind of blessing billion times more than a man, since man was created by God.*

'To invoke' literally means to make a request with special words for help to God Almighty. This kind of prayer by the way of invoking is the greatest prayer. And one, who can make such kind of prayer, will certainly find a positive response from God. The above-mentioned verse of the Quran gives a person this kind of assurance regarding his prayer.

There are two kinds of prayers: One, ordinary prayer or ordinary *dua*; the second, *dua* or prayer by the way of invoking God. The first kind of *dua* is simply a recitation of some words, but the second kind of *dua* is full of sentiments, full of spirituality, and full of divine spirit. So, if the first kind of *dua* is a *dua*, then the second kind of *dua* is a super *dua*.

The first kind of *dua* can be made by only using the words of a dictionary, but the second kind of *dua* requires something more;

that is, a deep realization of God, high trust upon God, and great love and sentiments towards God. It is these kinds of qualities which enable one to make that kind of *dua* which is called super *dua*.

Ignore them Politely

Life is a series of different kinds of experiences, both good and bad. When we have a good experience, that suits us perfectly well, but what to do when we have some bad experience? The Quran gives us a very simple answer: Avoid any unpleasantness by remaining non-committal.

This principle is set forth in the chapter *Al-Muzzammil* (The Wrapped One) of the Quran. When the Prophet of Islam started his mission in Makkah in 610 AD, the situation was highly unfavourable. Often he faced unwanted situations, and at that juncture this verse was revealed in the Quran:

> Bear patiently with what they say, and ignore them politely. (73:10)

In such a predicament, patience is not a passive attitude; it demonstrates great wisdom. When you keep your patience, you are saving your time and energy. Being patient in a difficult situation means that if you sense that the other party is not in a responsive mood, you should adopt the principle of avoidance, give him an evasive reply and then proceed with your own affairs. It is only if you see that the other party is listening to you in earnest that you should present your point of view to them. This principle is very important in social life. Society is a combination of different kinds of people and the way we live our lives in society is very often determined not by our own choices but by the will of others. If you try to convince all the members of society of your wish to prevail, you will seldom succeed, so practice the art of doing what is possible and leaving what is impossible.

This is a sign of maturity. The mature person remains even-tempered in situations which are impossible for him to change. If it is possible to bring about a change in the situation, then try for change, but when change is not possible, simply adopt the formula of adjustment.

You should live by your own principles and let other people live by their own principles. This is maturity, this is adjustment, this is the positive way of life.

This formula is important not only in society but also in your family. In the domestic sphere, there are always occasions when you feel that you cannot convince other family members of the rectitude of your views. That is when you should follow this formula: For you, your way of thinking, and for me, mine.

Studies show that difference is a part of life. Everyone has a different mindset, everyone sees things from a different angle, and everyone has different tastes. It is almost impossible to bring about uniformity among people. Trying to establish uniformity is like trying to make the impossible possible.

In such a situation, adopting the above Quranic formula, 'Live and let live', which is based on a practical principle, is the only common sense solution. It means simply that you should live by your own principles and let other people live by their own principles. This is maturity, this is adjustment, this is the positive way of life.

'Ignore them politely' means deal with them in a positive manner. If the questions put to you are of a contentious nature, respond to them in an indirect way or simply change the subject. To change the subject is also a polite way of answering. This kind of answer shows maturity and a disciplined mind. Moreover, it is the sign of a strong personality.

Life in a State of Urgency

One of the most important teachings of the Quran concerns death. Death is the end of the life of every man and woman, but no one knows when it will come. The Quran refers to this fact in the chapter *Luqman* (Luqman):

> No soul knows what it will earn tomorrow, and no soul knows in what land it will die. Surely, God is all-knowing, all-aware. (31:34)

Death is like an individual earthquake. Everyone is doomed to die, but no one knows when he is going to face this fateful moment. Death means complete detachment from the present world. It is like compulsory eviction from the world he has built for himself.

This being so, everyone is living in a state of emergency. Every moment could be his last moment. Every breath may prove to be his last. At any time he may face the fatal verdict of destiny—he may reach the point of no return in his life.

This situation is very serious; it is a great teacher for every man and woman. It creates a new kind of ethics that is based on death. This concept, if taken as a living concept, may change the whole way of a person's life. It may indeed revolutionize the course of his life. It can bring about a sea change in every human being.

The concept of inevitable death makes you very sincere. It saves you from all kinds of distractions. It nullifies all kinds of lust and exploitation. It tells a person that negative planning is pointless because before its fulfilment, one may die—and death is for all eternity. One may think against his fellow men but no one has the power to fulfil his evil desires against others.

One positive contribution of death is that it compels you to live in contentment, and contentment is the only source of peace and a tension-free life. In fact, the desire for more and more is an outcome of unawareness about death and contentment is a result of awareness of this universal fact.

Death serves as a regulator of life. Death serves as a positive teacher of every human being. The concept of death controls desires. Death enables one to live a healthy and constructive life.

The concept of death serves as a speed breaker in one's life. Death makes people adopt a realistic approach. Death reminds one of one's limitations. Death dispels all those negative desires, death is like a corrective measure in one's life, the concept of death serves as a check and balance force in life.

Death serves as a regulator of life. Death serves as a positive teacher of every human being. The concept of death controls desires. Death enables one to live a healthy and constructive life.

The concept of death compulsorily makes you live a purposeful life, it makes you set your target and priorities, and then exert all your energy and time for that target. One who is aware of the reality of death, cannot afford to live a purposeless life. Death is not a negative event in one's life; it has a completely positive lesson.

Crux of the Quran

❧◦✸✸◦❧

*I*f you go through the Quran in quest of its central message—
or the crux of the scripture—you will certainly discover an
important point on which the Quran lays great emphasis, that
is, its concept of *falah*. There are other similar words used by
the Quran such as *fawz*, etc. Both *falah* and *fawz* mean success.
According to the Quran, the truly successful are those and only
those who are destined to find success in the Hereafter.

Two well-known terms are very helpful in understanding the
Quranic point of view. These terms are 'promotion' and 'break
in service'. After a long period of service, one is given promotion.
Promotion brings better salary and better perks. According to
the Quran, the day one dies is the final day when one receives
promotion.

In our present world, we have been given all kinds of natural
amenities and the best possible life support system. It is like mini-
Paradise in which all the things we have been given are there
to test us. One who proves, by his good behaviour, in such an
environment that he is fit be admitted to Paradise will be selected
and promoted to the eternal life of the next, ideal world.

This promotion is based on the record of the pre-death period
of life. The present world is also like a paradise, in that it has
all those good things which will be given in Paradise, the only
difference being that the present world is an imperfect paradise,
while the paradise to come will be perfect.

Those who will be selected for this promotion will be allowed
to settle in the Paradise of the next world, where all the desires
they had in this life will be fulfilled. This paradise is free of all

kinds of disadvantages and limitations, and the eligible entrants will be able to enjoy all the good things it offers for all eternity.

Then there is a rule in government service that is called 'break in service'. Anyone who does his job for up to ten years and more but then absents himself from his office without prior permission shall have to pay a heavy price for this, this being considered a 'break in service'. Such is the case of those who have failed to utilize the opportunities that were given to them in the present world. This failure will be treated as break in service and the ruling will never be overturned. Defaulters will therefore enter the next world without any kind of favour and they will never have another chance to start their life again.

There is a verse in the Quran which says that the present world is very similar to Paradise. (47:6) Why is there this similarity? It stems from divine planning, for God Almighty wants only those who are truly deserving to find a place in the eternal Paradise. He therefore created the present world with many similarities to Paradise, so that He should know who measures up to the required paradisiacal standard in the way they live their lives in the present world. Then He will select those who pass the divine test in this life for settlement in the coming paradise—that is, the ideal paradise.

This is an idea which makes one very prudent about one's behaviour in this world.